To Susannah

With best wishes —

Will Parsons

D1342056

TANTRUMS AND TALENT

HOW TO GET THE BEST FROM CREATIVE PEOPLE

WINSTON FLETCHER

TANTRUMS AND TALENT

HOW TO GET THE BEST FROM CREATIVE PEOPLE

WINSTON FLETCHER

A completely updated edition of the pioneering management classic *Creative People*

Admap

First published 1999

Admap Publications
Farm Road, Henley-on-Thames
Oxfordshire RG9 1EJ, United Kingdom
Telephone: +44 (0) 1491 411000
Facsimile: +44 (0) 1491 571188
E-mail: admap@ntc.co.uk

A CIP catalogue record for this book is
available from the British Library

ISBN 1 84116 050 4

Typeset in 10.5/13pt Sabon by Admap Publications
Printed and bound in Great Britain by
Biddles Ltd, Guildford and King's Lynn

Contents

In memory of Talulah Gosh

There is an unbridgeable gap between the logic of business management and the laws of the creative world. The art of managing a creative group is to ensure that the conditions are as conducive to good work as they can be, and only then to apply the rules of efficiency. For efficiency is the enemy of originality and it can smother talent, which is of its nature non-conformist ... this is a lesson which the McKinseys of this world will not learn, and perhaps cannot learn!

Sir Denis Forman
Chairman, Granada Television (1974–1987)

Setting the Scene

What is creativity? Are highly creative people really different from everyone else? Or do they just pretend to be? How do they manage to conjure up new ideas – for songs, advertisements, stories, designs, fashions, television programmes or whatever – just like that, out of thin air, whenever they have to? Why are they so egotistical, temperamental and undisciplined? What drives them on? Ambition? Money? Fame? Self-fulfilment? How can they be motivated, managed and controlled? How can their creativity be optimised within organisational disciplines and constraints?

Tantrums and Talent (previously titled *Creative People*) is about the subtle, sensitive and often stormy relationships between those people who earn their living by selling their creative talents to organisations, and the organisations which employ them. Many of those organisations are vast bureaucracies – companies, industries and sometimes governments – ill-equipped to cope with the wayward ways of creative people, yet dependent on them for the creative products they offer the public.

Today's society consumes creativity voraciously. We watch television and hire videos; buy records and tapes; wear fashions; read magazines, newspapers and books; purchase furnishing and fabric designs; go to the cinema; switch on the radio; play increasingly sophisticated computer games; gaze at photographs and buildings and packages on shelves; and are incessantly cajoled by advertisements. Creativity which we have bought, or indirectly paid for, is with us every moment of the day. It permeates almost every aspect of our lives. It is produced in vast quantities, by vast industries, making vast amounts of money.

In the United States entertainment – the quintessential creative industry – now accounts for 5.4% of household spending, more than clothes or even health care. In the UK more people are employed today in the creative industries than were employed in the coal mines in their heyday.

Creativity is, however, utterly unlike any other product or service we consume. All other goods and services can be, and are, produced to formulae, often manufactured by robots, supervised by microchips, on production lines. Creativity cannot be mechanically mass-produced. Each and every creative idea comes into existence in a human mind. That will never change. Despite the wilder fantasies of science fiction,

1

machines – no matter how sophisticated – will never have ideas. So that organisations which depend on creativity will continue to depend, forever, upon creative individuals; and upon managing them successfully.

Managers, however, are not patrons of the arts. They are not buying for themselves. They are paying the creative people to produce work which they believe others – usually the general public – will like and want to buy. They are middle men. They must be loyal both to their customers, who pay them, and to the creative people, who produce for them. It is not an easy role to fulfil, and it is not made any easier by the fact that many creative people continuously suspect that the managers are like leeches, living off their talents, creaming off fat salaries for doing precious little.

Less than 40 years ago, the word creativity could not be found in leading dictionaries. Today creativity is one of the most fashionable words, and one of the most fashionable concepts in our society. Governments, businesses, educationalists, institutions of all kinds worship at its shrine. Tony Blair's words echo almost universally held views:

> Our aim must be to create a nation where the creative talents of all the people are used to build a true enterprise economy for the twenty-first century – where we compete on brains, not brawn.

The Prime Minister clearly intended to encompass creativity in both the sciences and the arts (as well as within every other walk of life). But in this book I shall focus solely on the arts, particularly on the commercial arts. That is not because I do not think science demands creativity. On the contrary, scientists are manifestly among the most exceptionally creative and original of thinkers. Anybody stupid enough to suggest that Newton, Faraday, Darwin and Einstein were not every bit as creative as Shakespeare, Da Vinci, Mozart and Tolstoy – though how can creativity be scientifically measured? – should stop reading now. And many of the challenges involved in the management of scientists in corporate organisations are much the same as the challenges involved in managing artists in organisations. But contrary to conventional wisdom, for reasons that will become apparent throughout the book, I do not believe the nature of creativity in the sciences is precisely the same as creativity in the arts. So that although some of the conclusions reached in *Tantrums and Talent* may happen to apply equally to both science-based and arts-based operations, I have concentrated on the latter. To have attempted to embrace both massive areas of activity would have just about doubled the book's length. More to the point, while I have a fair amount of personal experience in the management of creative arts people I have no experience whatsoever of managing creative scientists.

A country's commercial arts are sometimes called its 'culture'. That is the way the word 'culture' is at present used, for example, by the arts sections of several newspapers. But a nation's 'culture' comprises so much more than the arts such as its heritage, its customs, its shared beliefs and its language. I therefore prefer to use 'commercial arts' as the descriptor of the particular aspects of culture which we will be spotlighting.

What is the origin of the, comparatively recent, onrush of demand for creativity? Not everything that we want needs to be new. Many if not most of humanity's most basic urges and activities have changed little if at all over the centuries. (Even our trendiest sexual high jinks would teach little to the Greeks or Romans.) For some reason, which nobody has yet explained, most of us don't mind eating much the same meat or chocolate, or drinking much the same tea or coffee – or Coke or Johnnie Walker – again and again, week after week, with little or no variation from year to year. We may eat rather less beef or drink rather more coffee than we did a decade ago – and we eat and drink the same ingredients in increasingly diverse ways – but changes are slow and habits die hard.

In other areas of life, however, change is endemic. We would not dream of watching exactly the same television programmes, reading exactly the same magazines, watching exactly the same films or even wearing exactly the same fashions, again and again, day after day, year after year. If we enjoy a Heineken in the evening we expect, indeed may demand, that it be consistent and taste the same every night of the year. Imagine watching the same episode of *Coronation Street* every night of the year. It is inconceivable. We may be willing to accept, or even enjoy, a small amount of repetition: we have favourite records, favourite books, favourite films that we like to revisit from time to time. But even our favourites cannot bear too many encores: variety is intrinsic to the enjoyment of the experience. That is why the creative industries are chained to the treadmill of continuous change.

To some extent this is a modern phenomenon. In days of yore, entertainments were so rare they could afford to be slightly more repetitive, fashions hardly altered, and people read the Bible so often they knew it by heart from Genesis to Revelations. Tradition was the basis for most human activity, as it still is in many societies. Devout Christians, Jews and Muslims adhere to established behaviour patterns like flowers bending towards the sun. But the majority of people, certainly in Western economies, crave variety, crave change – crave creativity.

Though the phenomenon may be new, it will not be transient. On the contrary, there can be no doubt that it will burgeon and grow more widespread. In his book *The Biology of Art* Professor Desmond Morris advances the hypothesis that creative activities are:

> Actions which, unlike most patterns of animal behaviour, are performed for their own sake rather than to attain some basic biological goal. They are 'activities for activities' sake', so to speak. They normally occur in animals which have all their survival problems under control, and have surplus nervous energies which require an outlet.

It could hardly be said that humanity has all its survival problems under control; but in the advanced economies at least, we unarguably have surplus nervous energies which require an outlet. Increasing affluence and increasing leisure will fuel our demands for ever more creativity. The creative industries will flourish.

Inevitably some will flourish more than others. The most successful will be those that are most adept at harnessing the talents of the creative people they employ, to produce the products and services their customers want.

There have been innumerable books and articles, speeches and theses dealing with the question of how to encourage and engender the seeds of creativity which germinate in every human being. That, at least in part, is the burden of Tony Blair's words: we must ensure that the country's educational and organisational processes squeeze every last ounce of creativity from everyone. But *Tantrums and Talent* is not about that. It is about squeezing every last ounce of creativity out of those human beings who are, seemingly naturally, especially creative. It is about raising the peaks, rather than boosting the average. It reflects more closely another of Tony Blair's clear views:

> In the twenty-first century we are going to see the world economy dominated by the exploitation of creative minds.

Perhaps because many of the creative industries are still comparatively young, astonishingly little has yet been written about the problems involved in the management of highly creative people. The previous edition of this book, written in the mid-1980s, was one of the first thorough attempts to rectify that omission. Before writing it, I naturally examined all of the small amount of published material on the subject. Since then a fair amount of new research has been carried out and published, and has been incorporated into this edition.

Much more importantly however, before writing the first edition I canvassed the views of some of the foremost managers of creativity in Britain. This seemed (and I believe proved) to be the best possible way of discovering the keys to effective creative management. For the first edition, the following people very generously gave up their time to help me in the endeavour (titles at time of original writing):

Tim Bell – Chairman, Lowe Bell Communications
Christopher Bland – Chairman, London Weekend Television
Michael Grade – Chief Executive, Channel 4 Television
Paul Hamlyn – Chairman, Octopus Publishing Group
Jeremy Isaacs – General Director, Royal Opera House
Wally Olins – Chairman, Wolff Olins
David Puttnam – Chairman, Enigma Productions

Before starting on this new edition I felt it would be desirable to obtain an additional international perspective, and so interviewed Chris Jones, Chief Executive of J Walter Thomson Worldwide. I also felt the pop music sector had previously been under represented and plugged this gap by interviewing Alan McGee, chairman of Creation.

Without the insights, wisdom and guidance of all of the above I could not have written, nor revised, this book. You will find quotations from all of them scattered liberally throughout the pages, and I should like to take this opportunity to express to them, once again, my unqualified gratitude.

In addition, when writing the first edition I was given generous help and advice by Richard Birtchnell of the Burton Group; Hy Smith of United International Pictures; Victor Ross, ex-Chairman of the *Reader's Digest*, and Rob Dickens of WEA Records.

Finally, I particularly wish to thank my daughter Amelia Fletcher, who was the first to point out to me the key – and little appreciated – differences between creativity and talent. The analysis of these differences is one of the important ways in which this edition differs from its predecessor.

Management is not, and never will be, a predictive science like physics; less still is it like engineering. ('Human engineering' is a fatuous phrase, implying a scientific causality that does not and never will exist.) Creative people being what they are, nobody will ever succeed in managing them unerringly. However, some managers are a great deal better at it than others. All management is difficult. The management of creative people raises its own very particular problems. The more profoundly these problems are understood, the more effectively they can be resolved.

One small but important apology. For simplicity and ease of reading, the book has been written in the male gender. That is, 'he' has been used throughout rather than 'he or she' which, when repeated frequently, is both tedious and awkward. The use of 'he' is not intended to be sexist, and is most definitely not intended to imply that men are in any way better than women at managing creativity. They aren't. If anything, the reverse is likely to prove to be the case over the next few decades. But unfortunately the English language provides no simple, or fair, solution to the pronoun problem.

1

The Business of Creativity

The end of the twentieth century might be dubbed 'The Age of Creativity'. Or perhaps more accurately, 'The Infancy of Creativity' as, now that it has gathered such momentum, it is difficult to imagine how its forward thrust could ever stop. According to the Department for Culture, Media and Sport, in 1997–98 Britain's creative industries generated annual revenues of around £50 billion and employed almost three-quarters of a million people:

	Esimated revenues £million	Employment
Advertising	4,000	96,000
Architecture	1,500	35,000
Arts and antiques	2,200	40,000
Crafts	400	25,000
Design	12,000	23,000
Designer fashion	600	11,500
Film	920	33,000
Leisure Software	930	30,000
Music	3,600	160,000
Performing arts	883	60,000
Publishing	16,300	125,000
Television and radio	6,400	63,500

Those figures are estimates and – the Department doubtless reflecting the Prime Minister's manifest zeal for the subject – probably err on the optimistic side. The figure of 96,000 people working in advertising, for example, is well above any I have ever seen before and even exceeds the Government's figure of 80,000, published in the *Annual Abstract of Statistics*, which itself is too great. On the other side of the equation, there are industries, or at least parts of industries, that the Department has inexplicably omitted from the list. Why have only 'designer' fashions been included? Even the most modest C&A frock needs to be created, and the total clothes industry is worth approximately £26,000 million. Why has the bulk of the furniture business been disregarded? Again, even a knockdown MFI wardrobe has to be carefully designed – and IKEA have proved how creatively it can be done. The advertising revenue estimate is inexplicably low. Unless professional photography has been included as a 'craft' it, too, has been lost, as have greetings cards of all kinds, now worth nearly £1,000 million. How has the Department treated industrial designers who work within major companies – car designers, in-house shop designers and many others?

Taking the pluses and minuses together, however, the Department's estimates provide a ballpark base which cannot be wildly wrong. And at a minimum £50 billion turnover the creative industries listed account for some 6% of the UK Gross National Product. (The similar US figure quoted earlier relates solely to the entertainment industries. The US total for all the creative industries must be well above 10%.)

Some of the sectors are all but completely new such as designer fashions and leisure software. Others, though long established, have lately been growing like lusty youngsters. Within publishing, now a five-century-old industry whose demise has been prophesied more often than Delia Smith has cooked hot dinners, the number of books published continues to rise year-by-year. In Britain alone 100,000 new titles are published annually, nearly double the number of the late 1980s. Still in publishing, the number of general interest magazines has likewise zoomed from 1,500 in the early 1980s to over 2,400 today, and new ones are being launched almost weekly. The film and television industries now employ more people than car manufacturing. Television is burgeoning, as more and more stations come on air; very soon the average home will be able to receive three hundred or more channels compared with four less than a generation ago. And radio, another medium whose demise has often been predicted, is growing – if anything – even more rapidly. Our rock musicians today earn more in foreign exchange than our steel industry and account for 20% of total world sales of recorded music.

Though some of the figures are imprecise, there can be little doubt the entire sector is expanding far more rapidly than the economy as a whole, both in financial terms and in terms of the number of people employed. The sector's share of the GNP must be growing apace. And as we'll see in the final chapter, financially, many of those working in the creative industries are sitting pretty plushly.

The raw material of all creative industries is people. The people frequently – but by no means always – need equipment to do their jobs, and occasionally the equipment is highly expensive. Increasingly people's mastery of equipment, as it becomes phenomenally sophisticated, is a facet of their creativity. (This is obviously true in the movie, music and leisure software industries; it is less true in, say, publishing and the crafts). So the number of people working in the creative industries is a rough indicator of the raw materials involved. Manifestly the 750,000 or so people in the above list are not all 'creative'. Each sector will also employ its essential ration of salespeople and secretaries, IT boffins and bureaucrats, filing clerks and financial controllers – let's hope they are not too creative – who happen to find themselves working in creative organisations but could equally well be working elsewhere. All of which incidentally highlights the fact that highly creative industries also provide employment to a host of less than highly creative people.

The precise number of those who, as it were, do the creating is unknown. That is, the artists and architects, the designers and art directors, the musicians and writers and the rest. (Nor is it always easy to demarcate which job functions are, and which are not, truly creative.) However, using advertising – where the figures are known – as a very rough guide, it seems likely that about 40% of the total number employed are personally creative: it is their job to originate the material – to have the ideas and then to execute them. That would provide us with an estimated workforce of around 300,000 actively creative people – those who are paid to create commercial artistic work – in Britain today. In any event it is probably safe to assume the figure is not less than 200,000 nor greater than half-a-million, which makes 300,000 a reasonable approximation. That is the raw material: just under 1% of the working population. The number is not vast, but the people are vastly influential. The purpose of this book is to answer the question: how can the output of those key 300,000 individuals be optimised?

The ways in which creative people are employed are many and various, and inevitably mirror the fragmented nature of the creative commercial arts. The industry splits into three basic types of organisation. First, those sectors where the great majority of creative people are freelance – that is, technically, self-employed. Films, music, book publishing and the performing arts all depend almost completely on freelance creative people – though the companies employing them are often quite large. Second, those sectors which are crowded with small independent companies most of whose creative staff are employed full-time but which themselves generally work on a project-by-project (freelance) basis: this group includes architecture, design, leisure software, some television and radio production. The remaining, third, sector comprises mostly sizeable companies with continuous business (well, more or less) employing their creative staff from cradle to grave (well, more or less). Advertising, crafts, designer fashions, newspaper and magazine publishing and the larger independent television companies plus the BBC mostly fall into this category – though in every case even large operations sub-contract a good deal of highly specialised executional work to freelances and tiny independent companies. The divisions are not watertight, but they define the outline structure of the industry.

It is difficult to think of any other important part of the economy with such a labyrinthine mish-mash of infrastructures. (Building is probably closest, but trails way behind.) Inevitably the diversity of structures mirrors the diversity of creative input required. The creative industries reflect the specialisation of labour at its most hair-splitting. I have broadly divided the hair-splitting into macro- and micro-specialisation.

At the macro-specialisation level the creative industries are divided by their basic product. That is, music, design, fashion, architecture, advertising and so on. At this level there is little interchange of creative people between one specialisation and another. It hardly needs saying that few, if any, professional musicians could be professional designers, few, if any, professional designers could be professional actors, few, if any, professional actors could be professional advertising copywriters (though Alec Guinness has been both – a very rare exception to prove the rule). At the macro-specialisation level the differences seem so great that the managers and creators concerned rarely see any similarity between their own activities and those of other sectors. Whereas in most walks of life managers and executives are well aware the issues they face are similar to those faced by other managers and executives in other industries – that, after all, is the basis of most management education – those who work in creative businesses tend to be entirely inward-looking. They are almost always obsessed with their own creative terrain. Executives in the music business do not think they share many management processes with executives in the movie business, nor that both share much with executives in advertising, publishing and fashion and the rest. That is why agglomerating the 'creative industry' raises difficulties. People think of themselves as working in music or the movies, in advertising, publishing or fashion, not as working in 'the creative industry'.

Naturally, it is my contention that though there are many differences, the management processes involved in all the creative industries have much in common. And that they are quite different from other economic sectors – indeed they are unique. If that were not the case this book would have patently no *raison d'être* and would be built on shifting sands.

The specialist differences are minimised at arts festivals, and at arts centres like the Barbican, where the managers have to undertake, promote and co-ordinate a plethora of different types of artistic event. Even here, however, the activities involved are far from all-embracing, and generally unite only the performing arts.

The macro-specialisations among creative people are easy to grasp. It is at the micro-specialisation level that the hair-splitting becomes truly tricky for the manager. 'Micro-specialisation' is where the creators, seemingly, do exactly the same thing as each other: they act, they write, they compose. But in the world of creativity individuals usually do the same things differently. That is what makes them creative. No two authors will write the same book, no two divas perform the same opera, no two directors make the same film, no two architects design the same building. Creativity is essentially a personal activity; that is why robots cannot mimic it. The people are their own raw material. To some degree each and every highly creative person owns an economic monopoly: their own talent. 'Goldcollar workers view their talents as an asset, as their own best investment,' claims Robert F Kelley, senior consultant at SRI International, Menlo Park, California, and author of *The Goldcollar Worker*. (Adam Smith, with customary prescience, first advanced the theory that the wealth of nations is dependent on the abilities of its people, and more recently economists like Becker (1976) and Mincer (1979) have greatly enlarged the theory of 'human capital' – which is not, of course, unique to the creative industries.)

While recognising and being fully conversant with the differences between individuals' talents, when dealing with micro-specialisations it is broadly in the manager's financial interest to minimise their importance, even to imply they do not exist. The differences, as was noted above, provide creative people with monopoly power, however small. Because nobody else acts, or paints, or sings, or writes quite like they do, they can attempt, like any monopolist, to fix their own prices. In response the manager must believe that nobody is indispensable, that others may do things differently but not necessarily worse. This dictates a delicate but vital relationship between managers and creators. The manager must simultaneously communicate an enthusiastic appreciation of the creator's unique talents while implicitly communicating that nobody is indispensable. The manager must combine flattery with firmness, praise with parsimoniousness.

The legendary Hollywood moguls, the myths say, were ruthless bastards to their underlings: all parsimony and no praise. But that isn't right. With the stars and directors they wanted they were charm incarnate, and ludicrously profligate. How else did the stars and directors get to be so rich? They exploited their monopoly powers – in business terms their box-office power – and the moguls could do damn all about it. That was then. Today most movie stars' fees are determined by a computerised system which is based on the average box-office take of their last three films. That is truly treating talent as a commodity.

Like any other buyer, managers of creative people need to know what raw material is available at all times, in what styles, and what qualities, and at what cost. Often they will need to be able to choose (or reject) instantly and instinctively. To be able to do so the manager must be sensitive to the most minute differences of skill and talent between one individual and another; the manager must be able to spot subtleties of style, tone and approach and be able to relate them to the particular demands of the particular job in hand. It is one of the creative manager's most fundamental and essential skills. To quote Jeremy Isaacs:

> In inviting them to do the job you've made your creative decision, which is which creator to work with. It's no use turning round afterwards and saying I didn't want this, I wanted something quite different.

This is one of the key ways in which the creative industry's management differs from management in other industries and businesses (including, in my view, scientific creativity, which generally operates on far longer time scales and is far less diverse).

Few creative people, naturally, have as much financial clout as movie stars. In any sector those who can pretty well dictate their own terms number but a tiny handful. The ballet epitomises the issues with particular clarity. At one end of the spectrum are the prima ballerinas, the virtuosos, the glittering star performers who dance like dreams and captivate audiences. They create, they innovate, they have productions built around them. And like all stars they can, within limits, write their own pay cheques.

At the other end of the spectrum is the *corps de ballet*. By definition, on stage the members of the *corps de ballet* have no individuality or at least they sink their individuality completely as they move in perfect, exquisite unison. While they are in the *corps de ballet* they must be automata, with exceptional dancing ability but no originality. If they are conspicuous they are not doing their job. And yet, in any of the world's major ballet companies, to be a member of the *corps de ballet* is a massive achievement. Of all the dancers around, only a minuscule number, the very finest, will get into a top *corps* – where, immediately, their individuality will be suppressed. And they will be paid a rack rate. Current salaries in Covent Garden's prestigious Royal Ballet run out at a hardly prestigious £30,000 a year. (Is this what they spent the best years of their lives training so long and so arduously for? The answer is both yes and no.)

The same is true for many of those in choruses, orchestras and plays. The salaries of orchestral players at the Royal Opera House are the same as those of the *corps de ballet*, a princely £30,000 a year. And innumerable designers working in studios, session musicians, byline-less writers and working craftsmen find themselves in not dissimilar situations. (My own, personal, best ever acting performance, at school, was exuberantly praised at the time in the local paper, which wrote 'some of the supporting cast were surprisingly good'. I still treasure the cutting.)

The reality is that there is a continuum of individual monopoly power in every creative industry, from the queen bees at the apex to the worker bees at the bottom. Between the prima ballerinas and the *corps de ballet* there is a spectrum of median dancers, some closer to the top, some closer to the bottom, some whose careers are waxing, some whose careers are waning. And that is equally true of actors, architects and advertising copywriters and all other macro-specialist sectors. It may be thought to be universally true, in all types of business. But there are crucial differences between the creative industries and others.

First, Princeton University President William Bowen has argued, in his seminal book *The Performing Arts* (co-authored with William J Baumol), that the cost of personal services – naturally including creative services – must inevitably rise faster than the rate of inflation. While technological advances can bring down the cost of manufactured goods, Bowen argues, there is no way to improve the productivity of a pianist playing Chopin or an actor playing Hamlet. So that technological advances can offset cost increases in many industries, but they hardly apply in the creative arena, and as a result creative costs will always grow faster than others. I believe Bowen has over-egged the argument, as the creator's costs usually constitute only a fraction of the total costs; even though the fraction will sometimes be a high one.

Second, even the most humble creators believe themselves to have special talents – and they have. Filing clerks, waiters, labourers and shoe salesmen (all jobs I have done, incidentally) may or may not enjoy their work, do their best, and perform to their maximum, but they almost never feel themselves to have been born into the job. In contrast every violinist, designer, writer and singer feels themself to be using their in-born, natural – God-given if you like – talent. They have a sense of vocation, however slight. They believe it is in their blood. So managers who crassly imply to creators that they are dispensable and interchangeable, however much it may be true, will fail to motivate and maximise their outputs. Every member of the *corps de ballet* sees herself as a ballerina; every orchestral violinist sees himself as a soloist, every spear carrier sees himself as a leading actor. (And often the same people have a walk-on role in one event but a star role in others. That does not happen elsewhere.)

This does not mean that the manager of creative people must never crack the whip. On the contrary, much of this book specifically spotlights the need to control and restrain creative people, and identifies when, where and how. And the threat of dismissal, overt or covert, often underlies a manager's ability to bring creative people (like every other employee) to heel. The threat of dismissal is an implicit denial of the creator's monopoly power: the manager is saying 'you may think you are unique but I know I can find somebody else to do the job. Your raw material is widely available on the open market'.

Once this stage has been reached all hope of successful management has broken down, and it probably does not greatly matter to the manager what the employee thinks and feels. (Though there is never any need for the manager to be gratuitously nasty – nor should managers ever forget that creative worlds tend to be small worlds, where gossip is rife.) Before the final fracture, however, the manager must always keep in mind that creators believe their talents to be unique, no matter how minimally.

One of the commercial benefits, from the managers' perspective, of the huge diversity of employee relationships is that the raw material cost of creativity is highly sensitive to supply and demand. Managers rarely see it that way. When a teenage pop-idol's booty or an advertising copywriter's danegeld seem grotesque to any manager with a puritan view of life, it is vital to keep in mind that the laws of supply and demand operate more freely in the creative industries than almost anywhere else. In the UK, with a couple of exceptions, creators' trade unions are either weak or non-existent and the markets operate freely. There are armies of would-be raw material suppliers and, in most cases, an unusually large number of buyers needing to acquire vast quantities of raw material – though it rarely seems like that to the sellers. In every sphere of commercial creativity, from pop-music to fashion, from script-writing to photography, hosts of individual creators are clamouring for work; and there is always a prodigious number of projects available. In consequence the spectrum of earnings is bewilderingly wide: from the novice's pittance to the star performer's bullion. With innumerable buyers and sellers constantly negotiating, the competitive market determines the price for the job.

This is partly because no other industry produces and offers such an unimaginable variety of products or services to the public. There may be hundreds of cheeses on the market, and even more cars, and still more wines. But for diversity, no other field even starts to compare with the creative industries. As we saw earlier, 100,000 new books are published each year in Britain; plus 2,400 magazines, each coming out weekly or monthly and each jam-packed with different features and illustrations.

Over 40,000 hours of television are transmitted in twelve months, on the terrestrial channels alone, and even if only half of that is new material it equates to about 30,000 different programmes. Some 11,000 television commercials are produced each year, and nobody knows how many print ads, but the figure is usually taken as 25,000,000 (though I believe that to be an underestimate). Films, plays, gigs, concerts? The total must run into hundreds of thousands. New buildings? At least 150,000 are started each year. Fashions? The choice is almost literally infinite. And so it goes on ... records and tapes, radio transmissions, furniture and fabrics, packaging, leisure software, you name it. The variety of output of the 300,000 or so creators is mighty to behold.

This gives the public an almost indigestible welter of choice. Nonetheless, paradoxically, in a very real sense all of the creative industries are over-supplied. Each and every sector is crowded with eager creators offering their wares. All of them are buyers' markets. The world is swarming with aspiring authors, musicians, actors, film-makers, fashion designers, singers and everything else that might remotely be dubbed creative. Nor are all of them young hopefuls. Many are experienced professionals, unable to get more than a fraction of their desired output into production. Despite the huge volume of material produced and ceaselessly disseminated, much, much more fails to get executed (except by its creator) and fails to get disseminated. For example, about 45,000 new scripts are submitted in Hollywood each year, of which 200 become films. That means 224 out of every 225 scripts end up in the script editor's waste bin. The immensely successful writer Christopher Hampton has written more than 30 complete film scripts of which only 10 have been produced.

Many of those who feel irresistibly driven to create are not principally interested in the money, at least not at first. They will, and do, work for a meagre pittance, often for nothing. They want to do what they want to do. That, again, differentiates creative work from other work. Novices may offer their services gratis. Small independent arts production companies – I have been personally involved with several – earn little for their principals. They often make losses, and only just manage to keep afloat. Accountants call them 'lifestyle' companies. They offer their principals lifestyles they find amenable, but no riches.

This extraordinarily vigorous and competitive market puts, to be brutal, great power in the hands of the knowledgeable and courageous manager. The managers can, and frequently should, buy cheap raw material in the hope of getting a bargain. The artist providing the raw material may be cheap because it is unproven, or out of fashion, or is known to cock-up from time-to-time – or may desperately want the particular job, perhaps to enhance its career. Whatever the reason, the best creative managers consciously avoid playing safe all the time. They are adventurous. Employing the top talent, at top dollar, is generally the safe route artistically (even if not commercially, as higher costs will obviously be far more difficult to recoup.) Inevitably taking bold risks sometimes results in failure, and the manager must be prepared to take such failures on the chin. They go with the territory.

But throughout history those individuals who have been able to spot and nurture talent, taking control of talent which is young and cheap and guiding it towards riches and success, have themselves made fortunes. The process is most apparent in the pop music business – one instantly thinks of Brian Epstein and Alan McGee – but the same thing occurs constantly throughout the creative industries. Alchemists like Epstein and McGee are rare. But every good creative manager will forever be on the lookout for relatively undiscovered talent, which will offer new creativity, initially at bargain basement prices.

In the light of the uncertainties and financial risks, it is hardly surprising that managers in the creative industries have for years been searching for reliable rules and principles to help them predict the success or failure of new projects. Beyond establishing the most obvious truisms, their efforts have come to nought. Predictive market research occasionally has a role, as we will see in Chapter 10, but it is a small one. The past may provide rough guidelines for the future, but little more. The success of 'formula' soap operas and publications may, at first sight, appear to contradict this axiom. But even the most formulaic of creative projects demands constant inventiveness and originality within its 'formula'. (Just as, on a grander scale, great artists and musicians have managed to produce works of amazing originality within highly constricting disciplines.) Formula productions which lack continuous invention soon flop.

Do the creative industries provide goods, or services? Some make goods – books, magazines, newspapers, fashions, greetings cards, videos; others supply services – particularly entertainment, information and design. It has become common in the creative industries to describe individual projects, even within the service sectors, as 'products'. The managers and executives working on a film, or a television programme, or an advertisement, may refer to it as a 'product'. The creative people generally dislike this usage. They feel it belittles and demeans their work. Creativity is intangible, and ephemeral: how can it be a product? But nor do creators feel that they are simply providing a service – that, too sounds belittling. Nobody would describe Shakespeare's *King Lear* or Handel's *Messiah* as a service, nor Van Gogh's *Sunflowers* as a product, even though it palpably is one. Why, then, should a fashion design, or a radio play, or a pop song, or a television commercial be definable as a product or a service? This uncertainty about the status of creative output pinpoints yet another way in which it differs from other commercial and industrial activities.

All industries and organisations are creative in some measure and to some degree. Organisations which fail to adapt to changing circumstances, fail to meet and resolve challenges, fail to adopt new programmes, new plans and new products, soon wither and die. Most modern management theorists argue – and nobody disagrees – that creativity is an intrinsic and essential element in business success. As American management consultant Maurice Zeldman puts the accepted view:

> Creativity for organisations, like vitamins for people, is essential for good health and growth.

But creative industries are more extreme than others because the very things they produce and sell are 'creative'. Each 'product' is new, original, different from its predecessors, even if only marginally. 'Perishability is at the very heart of our business,' says Richard Birtchnell, then marketing director of The Burton Group. Other industries manufacture and market identical goods, continuously. That is usually what their customers want. Nobody wants every jar of Hellmann's Mayonnaise, every bottle of Guinness, every Mars Bar to be different: much the reverse. So while all successful organisations need to be creative, only those in the creative industries earn their keep by marketing things in a state of constant creative change.

Finally, while not denigrating the importance of detergents and pizzas, shampoos and handbags, washing machines and mobile phones, it is probably true that much of the output of the creative industries is today more fundamentally important and influential in society than the output of most other industries. Certainly that is what the creators think. And so do the managers.

> 'The good manager constantly stresses the relationship between creativity and society, the social responsibilities of the creative individual', says David Puttnam. 'The more creative the individual is, the greater that responsibility'.

Wally Olins, founder of Wolff Olins, concurs, and consciously reminds his creators of the importance of the work that they do in order to inspire them to stretch themselves:

> I try and explain to them the enormous significance of what they are doing, the enormous power that they have in the world, the fact that what they are doing is going to be seen by everybody, and it is their work. It is their imprint, if you like, on mankind. It may only be a very small imprint, but it is their imprint. I try to make them feel a sense of responsibility for what they are doing.

Few creators have the least doubt that the business in which they work is hugely important, and that what they are doing is hugely significant. They need to be sure the managers they work with share that conviction. That is a bedrock lesson in the management of creativity.

SUMMARY

- The creative industries are already huge and are growing faster than the economy as a whole.
- Their infrastructures are exceptionally complex and diverse.
- The raw material of all creative industries is people.
- The creative people who work in them seek to establish that their own talents provide them with personal monopolies.
- This is true of only a tiny handful of peak talents.
- The managers, in contrast, must generally establish the opposite: that virtually no creative person is indispensable. But managers must not let this view demotivate their creative people.
- The managers are helped by the vast over-supply of creative talent, and the resulting price competition.
- Managers therefore can and should take risks by employing 'inexpensive' creative people – and be ready to accept the inevitable occasional failures.
- For both creators and managers, recognition of the significance of their work in society is massively motivating.

2

What is Creativity?

We have got this far without attempting to define creativity. But then almost everyone instinctively believes they know what creativity is. Intuitively they agree with the design historian Stephen Bayley:

> Creativity is one of those things that is much easier to detect than to define.

He's right – and there are many such others: love, beauty, honour, truth, wisdom. Most, if not all, of the most significant words and concepts we use. (Asked to define science, the brilliant Nobel prize winning physicist J Robert Oppenheimer answered: *'Science is what scientists do'*. He too was right. And a very similar definition could apply to creativity.)

However we need to go a tad further than Bayley (and Oppenheimer). AS Reber's authoritative *Dictionary of Psychology* offers the following definition:

> A term used in the technical literature in basically the same way as in the popular, namely, to refer to mental processes that lead to solutions, ideas. conceptualisations, artistic forms, theories or products that are unique and novel.

More simply, the definition given by the UK Government's National Advisory Committee on Creative and Cultural Education runs:

> Imaginative activity fashioned so as to yield an outcome that is of value and original.

Neither definition seems perfect. The introduction of the word 'unique' into the dictionary definition causes difficulties. (If I have the same idea you had last week, without knowing you had it – which happens often in one form or another – is my idea not 'creative' too?) And the Advisory Committee's emphasis on 'value' seems altogether inappropriate. Throughout Britain, throughout the world, amateurs ceaselessly create music, art, poetry, not to mention gardens, toys and bits and bobs that will never have any value whatsoever, but unarguably are the result of creative effort. The quality of their creativity is beside the point.

I suggest the following brief definition will suffice:

Imaginative activity that yields an original or novel outcome.

This overcomes both the 'unique' and the 'value' difficulties – an idea may be original, even if it is no longer truly novel, and even if it has no value.

The concept of creation – making something out of nothing, bringing things into existence for the first time – has fascinated and perplexed humanity throughout the ages. All societies have their own myths to explain the creation of the world and the creation of mankind. Why? Because the notion that something can, magically as it were, evolve out of nothing is an affront to our experience, common sense and logic. If you want a chair you must start with wood, if you want a car you will need the metal, if you want some milk you must find a cow. But if you want an idea?

Almost throughout history, until very recently, it was generally accepted that ideas 'just happen', that they float into the mind of their own accord, unpredictably, and that no further explanation is possible, or is worth seeking. The paradigm example taught to every schoolchild is of Archimedes crying 'Eureka' as he discovered, in a flash, how the displacement of water explains the way things float. But the 'Eureka' description of creativity – sometimes called the 'Aha' theory – is highly deceptive, for two reasons.

First, it suggests that ideas arrive without prior cogitation. This rarely happens. Less than a couple of thousand years after Archimedes, Sir Isaac Newton was similarly struck, so the story goes, first by a falling apple and then by the theory of gravity. Neither the saga of Archimedes nor of Newton, in fairy-tale form, bothers to mention the crucial fact that both men had been brooding on the subject in question long and hard beforehand. When Newton was asked how he managed to surpass the discoveries of his predecessors he replied: *'By always thinking about them'*. One of the greatest creative mathematicians, Gauss, agreed:

If others would but reflect on mathematical truths as deeply and continuously as I have, they would make my discoveries.

Gauss's modesty was, in part, misplaced. Even if others had reflected as deeply and continuously as he did they are most unlikely to have made his discoveries. Diligence alone, diligence without ability, is insufficient. But so is ability without diligence. Had Gauss not stretched his mind so continuously he would have been a lesser mathematician. (For a marvellous exposition of the intensity and focus of a creative mathematician at work see *The Man Who Loved Only Numbers*, Paul Hoffman's delightful biography of the brilliant eccentric Paul Erdos).

Unwittingly, one of the most articulate proponents of the 'Eureka' school of creativity was Mozart. Being stupefyingly prolific and talented, he occasionally tried to analyse how he did it:

> When I feel well and in a good humour, or when I am taking a drive or walking after a good meal, or in the night when I cannot sleep, thoughts crowd into my mind as easily as you could wish. Whence and how do they come? I do not know and I have nothing to do with it. Those which please me, I keep in my head and hum them; at least others have told me that I do so. Once I have my theme, another melody comes, linking itself to the first one, in accordance with the needs of the composition as a whole.

Then, he continued, the whole work would *'stand almost complete and finished in my mind, so that I can survey it, like a fine picture or a beautiful statue, at a glance.'*

Faced with such potent creativity it is hardly surprising his envious rival Salieri believed Mozart to be in direct creative communion with God. However, it is important to note that Mozart was trained and driven by his father from childhood. And the thoughts which crowded into his mind generally did so only in response to a commission. Mozart composed his operas for cash, and worked immensely hard at them. He was a zealously meticulous worker. He seems never to have wasted any of the ideas that came to him. He moulded and remoulded his ideas into compositions until he found a perfect fit. But he had an astonishing musical memory, and so was able to construct major works in his head.

Like Newton, Gauss, and all the greatest creators, Mozart was born with immense talent which he honed and developed with immense perseverance – whether he realised this or not. In any event few, if any, other composers, artists and writers have enjoyed Mozart's seemingly effortless inspiration (though Shakespeare and Picasso must come close). Beethoven was, comparatively speaking, a plodder. Though he improvised with the fluency of a jazz musician, and some of his contemporaries considered his extemporaneous works superior to his compositions, his notebooks show he constantly jotted down themes and sketches, reworking and improving them arduously over many years.

Many composers are no great shakes at improvisation, many improvisers cannot compose. Many artists cannot sketch, many writers cannot instantly spin words. Nonetheless, the image of the artist as a uniquely gifted individual to whom inspirations come unbidden, from time to time, like bolts from the blue, is the one that has captured the public imagination. This is the 'Eureka' thesis in operation. Thomas Edison's famous contradictory dictum, that *genius is 1% inspiration and 99% perspiration* is widely quoted but not widely believed. Neither the public nor the creators themselves find Tchaikovsky's description of the creative process romantically attractive:

> There is no doubt that even the greatest musical geniuses have sometimes worked without inspiration. This guest does not always respond to the first invitation. We must always work, and a self-respecting artist must not fold his hands on the pretext that he is not in the mood.

And this leads to the second, and more fundamental way in which the 'Eureka' theory is misleading, particularly in the arts. It may, very occasionally, be an accurate description of what takes place in the sciences. Scientific discoveries, and scientific creativity, are sometimes dependent on a single perception or an *idea* – though even that is rare. (Einstein took at least ten years, from the age of 16 to 26, to develop his theory of relativity.) Artistic creativity is almost never a 'Eureka' phenomenon. This is yet another example of creativity in the sciences differing from creativity in the arts. That is not to say that ideas are unimportant in the arts – which would be nonsense, as we shall see. But the originality and creativity, of a work of art, of any kind, can rarely be described simply as an 'idea'.

The 'Eureka' theory implies that the vital, nay essential, quality in all creativity is the sudden inspiration, the discovery. And regrettably the 'Eureka' theory has percolated throughout the commercial arts, and taken hold. But writing a novel about an unfaithful Russian wife, or a play about a prince whose dad has been murdered by his mum's lover, or sculpting David, or painting a portrait of a lady with a quirky smile or of the battle of Guernica, or composing a symphony about the countryside are not inspired ideas. As ideas, indeed, they are rather dull. In none of those cases did the creativity did emanate from the *idea*. The creativity manifested itself in the execution and the handling of the idea.

Professor Robert Weisberg attempts to dissolve the dichotomy between ideas and execution by defining creativity as 'incremental' in nature. Because a great many artists develop and change their masterpieces as they progress, he concludes that the process comprises a series of discrete steps: a flight of separate, individual ideas. Perhaps it will one day be discovered that he is right, and that is indeed the way works of art are created. To me it seems unlikely. Once the initial idea has occurred the process is much less disjointed, much more continuous than Weisberg and most other theorists claim. Of course artists pause, or even down tools, from time to time, to consider and reconsider their progress; but in between pauses they work rapidly, ceaselessly, without stopping to think.

In management terms this point could hardly be more crucial. The creation of a successful play, movie, book, ballet, album, television series, building, advertising campaign, or anything else, will never be purely dependent on the 'idea'. Conventional wisdom dictates otherwise, but it is wrong. It is hardly an exaggeration to say that in the world of the commercial arts, ideas are two a penny. (That is one of the ways in which the market is hopelessly over-supplied: ideas are common as roses in summer). To make ideas succeed demands honing and polishing, working and reworking, time and diligence (and money). Above all it demands talent.

Talent is a word, and a notion, that is much undervalued in most analyses of creativity. This is probably because the Eureka theory is so pervasive, and has little place for talent. But talent is critical to the execution of creativity. An artist has to know exactly which brush strokes to place where; a writer has to select tens of thousands of words to write a book or play; a musician must have an aural sensitivity which guides him to select hundreds and hundreds of different notes – notes playing at the same time in harmonious counterpoint, and notes playing sequentially to make tunes. A film director needs to pick and manage the right crew and actors, an architect must know the structural and technical capabilities of the building materials, a fashion designer must be able to mould and cut fabric with flair. As those processes progress the creators will have numerous small 'ideas' along the way. But the processes themselves depend wholly and exclusively on talent – natural, inborn talent which has been educated by experience, and usually by training too. To quote the actor Eli Wallach, discussing creativity:

> When artists like Shostakovitch perform they don't say 'My finger has to go here'. They know they just have to play.

Talent is knowing precisely where your fingers have to go. When you work with top designers they will place a word or an icon in a particular spot on a blank page, and you can instantly see that is the right place, the exact place, the *only* place for it to go. That isn't an 'idea'. That's sheer talent.

Having sung the praises of talent, it is vital to add that (as with diligence) talent alone is never sufficient. Just as the creative world is crowded with people who have ideas but no talent, it is also crowded with people who have talent but no ideas. They are, if you like, the *corps de ballet* of the creative industries. Their gods, and their DNA, provided them with the ability to dance – or to write, draw or sing – but failed to go the whole hog. They have talent but no (or very little) originality. They know how to do everything but don't know what to do. Or if they do know what to do, what they do is pedestrian.

The nature of creativity then, particularly commercial artistic creativity, is that it is a process dependent upon diligence, ideas and talent. All three must be united. Any one of them alone will not produce *'imaginative activity that yields an original or novel outcome'* of any merit, or at least of any commercial worth. And that, for we are talking business here (and not just amateur creativity) is what the manager is there to generate.

However this analysis has still not explained how creativity comes about. And perhaps that should not be surprising. It was not until 1950, in an address at Pennsylvania State College, that the President of the American Psychological Association, J P Guilford, chose creativity as his theme *'with considerable hesitation, for it represents an area in which psychologists generally, whether they be angels or not, have feared to tread'*. Later in his talk, Guilford pointed out how neglected the study of creativity had been. Of approximately 121,000 books and papers listed in Psychological Abstracts in the previous 23 years, only 186 seemed to have any bearing on the subject of creativity: less than 0.2 per cent. Some 50 years later the percentage looks decidedly healthier. Nonetheless, in the spectrum of psychologists' interests and pre-occupations, creativity remains on the periphery.

Though the mathematician Henri Poincaré made a stab at it at the beginning of this century, the first determined attempt to provide a realistic theory of creativity must be credited to the great polymath Arthur Koestler, who – being both an accomplished novelist and a scientific scholar – was uniquely qualified to analyse the creative process. His seminal work, *The Act of Creation*, was published less than half-a-century ago and – though he unfortunately buys into the 'Eureka' theory hook, line and sinker – it is still the starting point to which anyone investigating the nature of creativity must first turn.

Koestler defined the process of creativity as 'bisociation': putting together two unconnected facts or ideas to form a single idea. (Koestler instinctively rejected the notion that ideas could materialise out of nowhere and nothing. Science teaches that changes occur to existing matter, even if they sometimes occur unpredictably – things do not come into existence miraculously.) Koestler contrasted bisociation with 'association'. Association refers to previously established connections between ideas, while bisociation involves the making of connections where none existed before. According to Koestler, every creative act involves such bisociative connections, and he justified his theory with many examples from the history of science.

In particular Koestler, building upon the Freudian theory of the subconscious, argued that the creative mind will mull over a problem unconsciously, until perchance it comes across a new and apparently irrelevant piece of information which locks into the problem – even though there is no logical reason for it to do so. The creative mind then 'bisociates' the new information with the (subconscious) problem and provides a solution:

> I have coined the term 'bisociation' in order to make a distinction between the routine skills of thinking on a single 'plane', as it were, and the creative act, which, as I shall try to show, always operates on more than one plane. The former may be called single-minded, the latter a double-minded, transitory state of unstable equilibrium where the balance of both emotion and thought is disturbed.

It is worth noting that Koestler assumed that creativity inevitably involved instability, and the disturbance of both emotion and thought.

While Koestler's theory of bisociation works well to explain such great scientific discoveries as Gutenberg and the printing press, Alexander Fleming and penicillin, Archimedes and flotation, and even Newton and gravity, it seems much less relevant when applied to the world of the arts. 'Bisociation' is no explanation for the inspiration of Mozart's works – any more than it could be for *Hamlet* or the *Mona Lisa*. The idea for the composition, the melody, or the plot, might in some way have been the result of bisociation; but the texture and richness of the work is, as we have seen, sheer artistry – and the theory of bisociation is altogether too rational to explain it.

At about the same time that Koestler was developing his theory of bisociation in Britain, a good deal of fundamental research into creativity was being carried out in the United States. Thrown into pandemonium by Russia's lead in the space race, Americans feared that they might be falling behind in scientific creativity. This gave great impetus to a burgeoning of research into the functioning of the brain. Brain specialists had long known that the brain is divided into two halves, left and right. But it was the pioneering work of neurosurgeons Philip Vogel and Joseph Bogen at the California Institute of Technology in the 1960s which established that the two halves operate quite differently, and perhaps even separately, from each other.

Having established that the two halves of the brain are biologically similar, Vogel and Bogen recognised that they can more realistically be thought of as two independent brains working in harmony than as a single brain divided into two, because each half-brain carries out different functions – functions the other half-brain has no idea how to perform. In general, the left-hand brain handles 'logical' thinking (eg, mathematics, language, analysis, deductions, logic), the right-hand brain 'creative' thinking (eg, imagination, colour, music, rhythm, daydreaming).

Work by Professor Robert Ornstein at the University of California also found that people who were trained to use one side of their brain more or less exclusively were relatively unable to use the other. Theorists then postulated that creative people are those who use the right halves of their brains intensively, while the rest of us coast along using the left halves. And that theory is now widely quoted and accepted, though more recent brain mapping analyses suggest that it is far too simple a picture.

Over recent years a good deal of experimental research has confirmed that the two halves of the brain can and do work independently – even to the point of continuing to function when they have been surgically severed. However, strong doubt has been cast upon the neat left/right division of abilities. In particular, researcher Michael Gazzaniga, who was involved in the original investigations into split-brain activity, has carried out what he calls 'a debunking of left-brain/right-brain mania'. He writes:

> Special talents can reside in the right or the left brain. Clearly, what is important is not so much where things are located, but that specific brain systems handle specific tasks.

In other words, the creative functions are separate from the logical functions, but neither will always be found, in all human beings, to the left or to the right.

Other theorists have developed more specific theories of creativity, all of which reflect, to some degree, Koestler's theory of bisociation, and the left versus right brain division. Lateral thinking, the concept of creativity invented by Edward de Bono, relates closely to Professor Ornstein's research. Lateral thinking, de Bono claims, consists of sideways leaps of the imagination (right brain activity), as contrasted with vertical thinking, the continuous progression down a logical chain (left brain activity). De Bono sums up the differences as follows: 'vertical thinking chooses, looks for what is right, maintains that one thing must follow directly from another, concentrates on relevance, and moves in the most likely direction … lateral thinking changes, looks for what is different, makes deliberate jumps, welcomes chance intrusions, and explores the least likely.'

In de Bono's words, you can stimulate lateral thinking if you deliberately 'arrange discontinuity'. However, his theories apply principally to the generation of ideas among non-creative people, rather than to the management and control of ideas among highly creative people – as does another much publicised theory of creativity, synectics.

Synectics is not really a theory of creativity at all, but derives from the 'brainstorming' approach to idea generation first invented by an advertising man, Alex F Osborn, in the 1930s and popularised by Osborn and Sidney J Parnes in the 1950s. Synectics itself was the brainchild of William J Gordon, who had worked with Osborn but saw flaws in the brainstorming concept. The word synectics, which comes from Greek, means the joining together of different and apparently irrelevant elements. Gordon identified the *underlying, non-rational, free-associative concepts that flow under the articulated surface of phenomena'*, and in a notable description of Eureka-type creativity, he wrote:

> It is the function of the mind, when presented with a problem, to attempt to make the strange familiar by means of analysis. The human organism is basically conservative and any strange thing is threatening to it. When faced with strangeness, the mind attempts to engorge this strangeness by forcing it into an acceptable pattern or changing its private geometry to make room for the strangeness … But basic novelty demands a fresh viewpoint, a new way of looking at the problem. Most problems are not new. The challenge is to view the problem in a new way. This new viewpoint in turn embodies the potential for a new basic solution.

From the standpoint of the management of creativity, the essential conclusion to be drawn from all these analyses is that despite their differences the theorists unanimously agree on one thing: not only are logic and creativity different mental processes, they are generally in conflict.

Bisociation is the antithesis of association; lateral thinking is the antithesis of vertical thinking. Whether or not they are to be found on the left or on the right, creativity and rationality occur in different parts of the brain. At times of creation, all the theories agree, logic must make itself scarce. Logic, of course, must not be confused with diligence. It is implicit in Koestler, de Bono and others that creativity does not exist in a vacuum. Creativity blossoms only in well tilled and fertilised soil. A period of incubation is a pre-requisite, before a new idea can be born. To quote the great rationalist and philosopher Bertrand Russell:

Having, by a time of very intense concentration, planted the problem in my subconscious, it would germinate underground until, suddenly, the solution emerged with blinding clarity, so that it only remained to write down what had happened as if in a revelation.

This is an experience which everyone who has ever forced themselves to solve intractable problems – whether in business, science or the arts – will recognise. To some extent it is a technique that can be learned. In youth (speaking for myself at least) one feels it necessary to resolve every problem as it presents itself. Later on, one gains the confidence to know that certain problems can best be left to simmer on a mental backburner, and that the mind will serve up the solution when it is ready – provided that one has thought hard about the problem and is not merely procrastinating. As long ago as 1926 the psychologist G Wallas hypothesised that thought processes can be divided into four stages: preparation; incubation; illumination and verification. (Others have added an intervening, additional period: frustration, which occurs when all the preparation has been done, but the solution remains infuriatingly elusive.)

If much of the above sounds rather dour and forbidding, it is perhaps worth ending this chapter with this delightful quote from the film director Henry Jaglom, who described the joys of creativity as like *'being on a bicycle going downhill'*. Well, sometimes.

Creativity depends on ideas, diligence and talent. Ideas and talent can rarely if ever be explained and defended rationally. The instincts that tell a designer which typeface to use, a copywriter which phrase to employ, a pop singer which notes to choose, can never be elucidated entirely logically. In contrast, management is – or at least desperately aims to be – quintessentially rational. And this means that there is an underlying and unavoidable clash of cultures and processes when managers find themselves in control of creativity. A clash of cultures often exacerbated, as we shall see, by the nature and personality of creative people themselves.

SUMMARY

- Creativity may be defined as: 'Imaginative activity that yields an original or novel outcome.'
- Most explanations of creativity concentrate on the 'Eureka' theory, on the origination of ideas.
- The 'Eureka' theory of creativity is misleading and deceptive, particularly with regard to artistic creativity. (It has just a smidgen more validity in the sciences.)

- Creativity demands diligence, ideas and talent. None of those alone, nor any two of them alone, are likely to produce creativity of merit.
- All theories about the nature of creativity accept, at their basis, that creativity and logic are in many ways inimical to each other.
- Because managers are trained, and expected, to be logical in business analysis and decision-making they find the management of creativity especially difficult.

3

The Creative Personality

Most of us have, in our mind's eye, an image of the typical creative genius. He will probably be a synthesis of Vincent Van Gogh, Albert Einstein, Dylan Thomas, Lord Byron, Paul Gauguin and James Joyce.

The qualities represented by this photofit prodigy include extraordinary intelligence, absentmindedness, commitment, introversion, volatility bordering upon (and often lapsing into) madness, too much liking for the hard stuff – and above all an egocentricity so powerful that it can disregard, not to say despise, the attitudes and opinions of the rest of society. Inevitably some aspects of this glamorous image rub off onto the commercial creative person. How far is this justified?

Start any conversation about the true character of artists and you can safely bet an original Rembrandt to a chocolate box cover that within five minutes somebody will mention either Van Gogh, or Gauguin, or both. Why? Not because they are typical, but because they are atypical. They epitomise the way we like our artists to be, the romantic ideal. But not a lot of artists either amputate their ears or dash off to Tahiti; not a lot destroy their lives in the blind, passionate pursuit of their art; by comparison at least, most artists live reasonably conventional existences.

Nonetheless, creative people are not quite like the rest of us. It is a difficult area to research, but during the last few decades a succession of independent studies have established clear correlations between creativity and personality. An authoritative study by Jacob Getzels and Mihaly Csikszentmihalyi, at the Art Institute of Chicago, which compared art students with the general college population, showed the art students to be more socially aloof, introspective, self-sufficient, radical, experimental and nonconformist – reflecting reasonably accurately the popular stereotype.

Another study, by H J Walberg, a researcher specialising in creativity, suggests that young, creative students find books more interesting than people, are interested in work with fine detail and show greater persistence than others in carrying things through. They feel themselves to be more imaginative, curious and expressive. In choosing the best characteristics to develop in life they select 'creativity' more often and 'wealth and power' less often – all of which confirms their view of creativity as a vocation.

Significantly, Walberg's study also suggests that the personalities of creative artists and scientists differ. The scientists rated intelligence higher than creativity; they had more difficulty relating to other people; they were better at continuing to work despite distractions and were 'control freaks' – they made detailed future plans for themselves, while the young artists were disposed to let fate take its course. Walberg concludes:

> The differences found imply that communicated inner feeling is the essential preoccupation of the artist (Beauty), whereas single-minded conceptual grappling with external realities is the *sine qua non* of science (Truth).

In no study have the differences between the creative students, artists or scientists, and the remainder of the sample – the less creative respondents – been vast. If you draw a spectrum from extreme conformity at one end to extreme non-conformity at the other, creative people will veer towards non-conformity. A few, like Van Gogh and Gauguin (and Einstein, who was decidedly eccentric), will be far out on the extreme edge. The great majority will differ from the norm in less dramatic ways.

To quote Michael Badawy, professor of technical management and applied behavioural sciences at Virginia Polytechnic Institute, in his perceptive essay 'How to Prevent Creativity Mismanagement':

> Creativity is like height, weight and strength. People vary considerably in these dimensions, but everybody has some height, some weight and some strength. Likewise, there is a certain amount of creativity in all of us, but some of us are obviously more creative than others.

Chris Jones of J Walter Thompson puts the same point slightly differently:

> It's almost a physical thing. We can all run and jump, but some people can run faster or jump higher.

And the differences are sufficiently important for the manager to be constantly aware of them, and take account of them. To quote Professor Badaway again:

> Many managers do not apply (or even sometimes misapply) what behavioural scientists have learned about creativity and creative environments. This leads to mismanagement and poor results. Managers

seem to do more to stifle creativity than to induce it. The most common mistake managers make is to attempt to manage highly creative individuals using the same standards they apply to the more conventional members of the work team.

Christopher Bland, now Chairman of the BBC, expresses the differences thus:

> They start out differently, and their imperatives are different too. Not that they're all the same. But in terms of what interests them and what drives them, plainly they are different to ordinary people. They don't, in many cases, care about making money, either for the company, or sometimes even for themselves. And that is a distinction between them and the ordinary manager of an iron foundry. He's really in the business of making money. No doubt he wants to make decent castings as well, but it's in that order.

Tim Bell, Chairman of Chime Communications, shares Bland's view:

> Their motivations are different, their objectives are different and their attitudes are different. It's a bizarre thought, but the fact that they look different suggests that they are different. They don't like wearing suits, they like looking scruffy, they like to wear whatever the latest fashion is. They don't like offices with desks and filing cabinets and traditional office furniture. They're not commercial, yet they're in highly commercial businesses. They are different in the way they approach life.

Sigmund Freud – himself no mean creative thinker – thought these differences could be explained by the fact that the urge to create is caused by frustration, because all creativity involves fantasy and 'a happy person never fantasies, only an unsatisfied one'. He felt creativity to be a substitute for other, more normal activities and therefore deduced that it resulted from neuroses and failure. Today, few if any analysts of creativity accept Freud's thesis in its entirety – though the adage 'out of pain cometh great art' is almost conventional wisdom and was certainly believed, for example, by Marcel Proust. And it is widely accepted that highly creative people are particularly insecure, in their relations both with themselves and with others.

While Freud argues that their insecurity is caused by frustration, those who work with creators offer a simpler explanation. As David Puttnam says:

> Basically creative people are people who are prepared to be judged by their output. That's a tremendously important decision in life: 'I did that –

do you think I'm worthy?' Creative people have a need to communicate or articulate their thoughts. That's important to them. And many of them have a need to entertain and to be appreciated. These are the differences which separate them out.

It is difficult to over-estimate the effect that 'being judged by their output' has on the creative personality. For many artists, writes Dr. Anthony Storr in *The Dynamics of Creation*:

> The work, rather than the person, becomes the focus of self esteem. To mind more about one's book or one's painting than one does about oneself will seem strange to those who are sure enough of themselves to be themselves in social relations. But if a book or a painting contains more of the real person than is ever shown in ordinary life, it is not surprising that the producer of it is hypersensitive.

I put Dr Storr's thesis to Alan McGee, and he concurred without demur. Describing the best pop musicians he added:

> Through their music they bare their souls. It's a form of obsession.

Chris Jones metaphorically compared creativity to parenthood:

> Their work is umbilically linked to them. It is hard to take criticism of your children without taking it personally.

Or as the French novelist Gustave Flaubert put it, still more graphically:

> A book is essentially organic, part of ourselves. We tear a length of gut from our bellies and serve it up.

Pure artists and commercial creative people are almost unique in the way that they are personally linked to their endeavours. (Politicians and sportspeople – who are also publicly 'judged by their output' – are similarly subject to the cult of the personality and often with similar psychological results.) The vast majority of the world's workers, in the vast majority of jobs, do their work anonymously. Individual's names are not affixed to their output. The identity of the people who built your car, or produced your bananas, will never be known to you. Nor to anyone, outside their organisation – and not even to many of those within.

Creators were not always thus associated with their work. In mediaeval times, when they were seen as craftsmen – factory workers, as it were – their often magnificent creations glorified God rather than themselves. Giotto never signed a painting. (The two on which his name appears are not believed to have been painted by him.) But today even the humble chorus and the *corps de ballet* are individually named in the programme. Every film, television and radio production begins and/or ends with the names of the actors, writer(s), director, producer(s) and all the subsidiary creative employees, many of them very lowly in the creative hierarchy. Journalists get bylines, photographers have their identities pressed hard against their pictures, architects and fashion designers become household names. How many can name the chairman of Unilever, or the chief executive of Ford, let alone the financial director of British Telecom or the production director of Shell?

While the names of the innumerable managers and executives who keep the wheels of industry turning are never seen in lights, creative names gleam and glitter, throughout the world. Indeed legislation gives certain creators, uniquely, the right to be identified whenever their work is published or is 'issued to the public'; and, also uniquely, gives them the right to object to 'derogatory' treatment of their work. ('Derogatory' here means any treatment which amounts to distortion or mutilation of the work, or is otherwise prejudicial to the honour or reputation of the creator.)

Indubitably creative people crave and enjoy fame. Sigmund Freud considered it to be one of their essential drives. But the reverse side of the coin of fame is blame. To be personally identified with your work when things go right is delightful: when thing go wrong it is dire. So it isn't only the creators themselves who want to be associated publicly with their work. It also suits those who employ them. Employers are well aware that this puts pressure on their creative employees to do their best. Thus the fame in which they bask fuels their insecurity and this carries profound implications for managers.

The fact that they are 'judged by their output' both exacerbates, and makes them dependent upon, their egotism. Numerous studies – including three by Coopersmith (1967), Garwood (1964) and Stasinos (1984) for example – show creative people to be particularly high in personal self-esteem. They listen to themselves more and are far more likely to trust their own judgments. They are much more influenced by their own, inner standards than by those of the society or profession to which they belong. In another study, among architects, in which the subjects were divided into three groups according to their creativity, the most creative group were primarily concerned with meeting a standard of excellence which they discovered within themselves; the least creative group with simply conforming to the standards of their profession.

In summary, these studies confirm that creative people are more independent, more self-reliant and more assertive than less creative people.

That is the nature, so to speak, of the beast. But from an organisation's point of view, assertive independence breeds several unfortunate by-products. Most creators are personally-driven rather than company-orientated. They tend to view gung-ho company loyalty with a suspicion bordering on disdain. Doubtless that is why so many of them are self-employed, and only offer their talents to employers on a freelance, job-by-job basis.

Also, assertive independence often shows itself as combative stubbornness, a trait commonly ascribed to creative people, though not necessarily unwelcome: *'If creative people believe they are right they must be stubborn about it,'* insists Paul Hamlyn, former Chairman of Octopus Publishing Group. Tim Bell agrees:

> The creative people who are the most difficult to get good work out of are the ones who want to please you. That's the wrong motivation. They should want to please themselves. That is the absolutely correct motivation. Stubbornness is fine. It is unreasonableness that's not. Stubbornness and unreasonableness are different things.

The problem of unreasonableness leads to the frequently questioned relationship between creativity and intelligence. Tim Bell in effect would like creators to show more intelligence in their assessment of their own work. But is it necessary to be intelligent in order to be creative, or – as is sometimes suggested – is exactly the opposite true?

In recent years it has become fashionable among psychologists to dissociate intelligence from creativity, to the point where it might be supposed that a high IQ is a bar to originality. And certainly anyone who has attended university will have met many academics who have immense intelligence but little or no imagination. The reality, as numerous studies have now established, is that there is no direct correlation between creativity and IQ, and IQ scores can never be used to predict creativity. However, almost all highly creative people have an IQ somewhat above average, often around 120. They are bright, but not outstandingly so. Professor Frank Barron summarises the situation:

> For certain intrinsically creative activities a specifiable minimum IQ is probably necessary, to engage in the activity at all, but beyond that minimum, which is often surprisingly low, creativity has little correlation with scores on IQ tests.

(These findings relate to artistic creativity, and may not apply to scientific creativity).

Once again we see the seeds of dissension between creativity and management. Senior managers are usually (though admittedly not invariably!) chosen for their intelligence, have an academic education, and have been trained to respect and respond to intellectual abilities. Lacking these particular abilities, the creative people may fall back upon stubbornness, and appear intransigent because they lack analytical debating skills.

The difficulties might be less pronounced if creators were better at editing their own work. But even the greatest artists often produce pap. Picasso's paintings and Shakespeare's sonnets are of variable quality, to put it generously, and even Leonardo da Vinci – rightly celebrated for a lifetime of astonishing creative achievement – had loads of daft ideas, including one for a machine which flew by flapping its wings, on which he worked enthusiastically for years. Nor is it merely the little ideas that great men frequently get wrong. Sir Isaac Newton spent a quarter of a century studying alchemy, and wrote thousands of more or less worthless pages on the subject; while his intellectual heir, Albert Einstein, rejected Max Planck's discovery of quantum mechanics saying, 'An inner voice tells me it is not the real thing.' This inconsistency in creative people's output and judgment is one of the most intractable problems which managers face. It is hard to think of any other group whose work varies so greatly or so unpredictably. Nobody doubts that on average (if such an average could ever be calculated) the most talented creative people produce high quality work more consistently than the least talented. That is the assumption upon which all creative fees and prices are based, and it is essential to the orderly working of the marketplace: 'He did a marvellous job last time, so the odds are he'll do a marvellous job next time.' It is a sound rule-of-thumb, but odds are not certainties. Outstanding creative people can and do charge more for their services because nine times out of ten they can be relied upon to produce outstanding work. Or might it be only six times out of ten? Time and again the most highly-talented and conscientious creators blunder, boob and botch things up; and just occasionally, to balance the equation, individuals of mediocre talent produce gems of immense worth.

In the management of creativity this patchiness of output is a constant problem. One of the manager's principal functions, for which he will in turn be reviled and then blessed, is to spot the creator's goofs before they go public. That is not easy when you are dealing with a top film director or architect. It isn't even easy with lesser, but equally passionate mortals. Having spotted the goof, the manager must then be able to convince the creator of its goofiness – which is more difficult still, and occasionally borders on the impossible. Putting right errant creators involves huge amounts of time, argument, resolution and guts: it is not a task for the impatient or the uncombative. It involves earning the creator's trust and confidence; sometimes it involves the deployment of contractual power and occasionally it finally results in an irrecoverable breakdown in the relationship.

Great creators bubble with ideas. They then, themselves, attempt to reject their dud ideas ruthlessly. (But they do not always recognise their dud ideas.) They also identify imperfect ideas which they feel have promise and persevere with them, for as long as it takes to get them right. Here, for example, is Robert Weisberg's description of Pablo Picasso's approach to the painting of his great mural, *Guernica*:

> Several possibilities for the general composition of the mural were considered before Picasso began to paint, and the composition underwent further changes while he painted. Likewise, specific aspects of the characters were considered again and again in preliminary work and then modified still further as the painting progressed. Picasso is very hard to satisfy and always ready to try once more to get some small detail a little better.

The same meticulous process is documented and portrayed in almost every author or composer's notebook, in every artist's sketchbook and in the drafting and re-drafting to which most of the world's greatest masterpieces have been subjected before they reach the public. Having themselves gone through this arduous process creators naturally feel that the end result is as perfect as they can make it and equally naturally they resist unenthusiastic responses from managers – people of whose creative judgment they are invariably unsure. (In the manner of that old saw 'If you're so clever why aren't you rich?', creators tend to think 'If you've got better creative judgment than me why can't you create?') Nor are managers always right, any more than creative people.

The editing of their own work reflects the commitment to perfection which is another fundamental aspect of the creative personality. Perfectionism, unfortunately, takes time and costs money. So an undisciplined dedication to its achievement inevitably brings creators into conflict with managers, one of whose most important job functions is the control of costs and time schedules. The paradox is that managers accept (and admire) creators' perfectionism; they recognise that perfectionism is an inherent and essential part of creativity; but they are rarely able to provide the resources necessary for its attainment. This dilemma will be explored fully in Chapter 8.

To achieve perfection creators put their heart and soul into their work. This aspect of the creative personality is one that conflicts with the conventional image of the artist as someone who lazes about nonchalantly, daydreaming, chatting, drinking, and having ideas from time to time, preferably in the bath ('Eureka!'). That image could hardly be less accurate. Biographical and psychological studies of creative people consistently prove they are driven by the compulsion to work and by the joys their endeavours bring them. (In the words of Nobel prize winning inventor Dennis Gabor 'Nobody has ever enjoyed science as much as Albert Einstein'.) And the degree of their commitment to their work appears to be another important difference between creative and non-creative people. A simplistic explanation would be that creative people enjoy their work more than others – it can sometimes, after all, be like cycling downhill. Nonetheless, as we saw in the previous chapter, creative people often need to force themselves to work. All that can be said with certainty it is that they prefer creating, difficult and painful though it often is, to doing anything else.

The final aspect of the creative personality – a consequence of the radicalism and non-conformity identified by Getzels and Csikszentmihalyi – is rebelliousness. Since new thoughts and ideas can only be brought into existence by those who question existing ones, it is hardly surprising that a spirit of rebelliousness should be endemic to creativity. Freud, perhaps predictably, suggests that this rebelliousness against the past is an expression of artists' hostility to their parents – a hostility which, he believes, engenders artistic creation. However, rebelliousness of itself is obviously no guarantee of creativity. To quote Stephen Bayley again:

> Creative people need to have a sort of vision and a strong moral commitment to changing things for the better. They have to be unafraid of breaking rules, although it's axiomatic they have to know the rules in the first place. So they have to be disciplined people.

Creators' innate rebelliousness inevitably leads them to dislike taking orders. Since most managers are in the habit of giving orders, however mildly stated, this is yet another aspect of the creative personality with which they find it difficult to cope.

Moreover, although the great majority of creators are not, as we have seen, uncontrollably wild, in every creative industry there will invariably be found a handful who are. And some of these (by no means all of them) may be the people with the greatest talent. It may well be (but how could it be proved?) that just as many bank clerks and garage mechanics would be equally uncontrollable and wild, were they ever allowed to be. Lacking unique creative talent, they either restrain themselves or end up locked-up. Because outstanding creative ability is so rare, the creative manager who employs talented people must learn to live with their tantrums. Christopher Bland says:

> It may be difficult, but does that mean you won't work with Callas? How likeable was Callas? By all accounts, not at all. The word prima donna comes from opera! To say you can only work with those you personally like – no, it would be impossible.

Paul Hamlyn agrees:

> Creative people are certainly more difficult, sometimes difficult in unpleasant ways. Some of the big, best-selling authors are pretty obnoxious. As people. But you put up with them.

Michael Grade agrees, too:

> If they've got talent I don't have to like them. I have to like their talent. I've worked with a lot of creative people I couldn't stand. They wouldn't know I couldn't stand them. They never know that.

And so does Tim Bell:

> It can be fantastically frustrating working with creators. They're petulant and difficult and refuse to pay attention and have different priorities. Dumb insolence is a classic characteristic of creative people and they are very dismissive of everybody else. The answer, then, is not to deal with them but to deal with their work. Liking them needn't come into it.

Nor does Christopher Bland find anything particularly untoward in this situation:

> Yes, you have got to be able and willing to work with outstanding talents you dislike. Otherwise you'd cut yourself off from a great deal of talent. If you only published authors you liked, and wanted to have dinner with, and go on holiday with, you'd have a very short list indeed. Why should great artists be likeable? Most of them are anything but, and to expect it I think is odd. Plainly it's a great bonus if they are.

We have seen then that creators tend to be egotistical, assertive, independent, rebellious, perfectionists who seek fame and are not necessarily all that highly intelligent. However, these diverse and often complex personality traits do not, even when added together, mean that creators are nutcases, with bats in the belfry and screws loose. Those creators who are, in some degree, mentally unbalanced, are a minuscule minority. Naturally, as with Van Gogh and Gauguin, they are the ones about whom well-worn and frequently apocryphal anecdotes are often told in pubs. But every scrap of available evidence shows that creativity and mental instability rarely go hand-in-hand. Indeed, the fact has been well-established since 1904 when Havelock Ellis (better known for his studies in the *Psychology of Sex*) published a book called *A Study of British Genius*. From the *Dictionary of National Biography*, Ellis culled the names of 1,030 'geniuses' among whom he could discover only 44 (4.2 per cent) who were demonstrably insane. He wrote, with evident regret: 'The association between genius and insanity is not, I believe, without significance, but in view of the fact that its occurrence is only demonstrable in less than five per cent of cases, means we must put out of court any theory of genius being a form of insanity.'

Ellis's figures, as Dr Anthony Storr points out in *The Dynamics of Creation*, are remarkably low since they include senile disorders; and the lack of any association between madness and creativity is emphasised by the fact that nowadays one in 15 of the British population (6.7 per cent) is resident in a mental hospital at some point in their lives. Dr Storr concludes: '*For creative work, access to the inner realm of the psyche is essential. But so is a strong, functioning ego, capable of judgment, inhibition of immediate impulse, persistence and control.*'

The same important point is made by Dr Jonathan Miller in *The Keys to Creativity*:

> There are artists who happen to have been depressed, frenzied or manic, and who also happen to be geniuses. But their genius does not flow from their disorder. It's something they manage to live with and to produce with. The idea that you have to be in some way disordered to produce, or that it's an advisable state of mind, is nonsense.

And referring to creators in business, Professor Carl Hakmiller, of the University of Connecticut, concurs:

> The myth of weirdoes running around wearing plaid shirts and no socks just isn't true.

It has been important to labour the fact that, no matter how difficult they may sometimes be, creative people are not a crazy, incomprehensible species, because it is a cliché that much appeals to some creators and to some managers. To the creators it is an excuse (indeed an encouragement) for capricious, selfish, histrionic behaviour. To the managers it explains why creative people are impossible to control, and provides a heaven-sent reason for being unable to deal with them.

To manage creative people successfully you must obviously understand their personality traits and idiosyncrasies. But it is equally important – if not more important – never to treat them as oddballs. Michael Grade, then Chief Executive of Channel 4 Television, gave this advice:

> When you're dealing with creative people's egocentricity or temperament you've got to ask yourself, 'Why are they like that?' And the answer is that they are in a very exposed position. They are therefore very insecure. If you understand their insecurities then you can deal with them. People aren't egocentric or temperamental for no reason, it's rarely a character flaw. We are all insecure in some ways, and our insecurities manifest themselves differently. Some of us are temperamental, some of us are depressive, some are bad at paperwork. And in each case you have to understand why. You have to understand what the job is you want the creators to do, and find a way to get the best out of them.

To the good manager that will all be basic common sense. But damn difficult to achieve.

SUMMARY

- Studies have shown that creative people have different personality traits from others.
- Among other things, they tend to be more independent, assertive, introspective, radical, experimental, non-conformist and high in self-esteem. (There are some differences between scientific and artistic creative people.)
- In general the differences, though noteworthy and significant, are not massive. Very few creative people have extreme personalities, even fewer are 'crazy'.
- Some creative people, and some managers, like to exaggerate creative peoples' idiosyncrasies, because it suits their purposes.
- Creative people are judged, and prefer to be judged, by their output rather than by their personality.

- They are usually identified with their output, by name, which is a requirement of their egotism, but is also of benefit to the manager.
- Their output is inevitably inconsistent, and it is the manager's role to correct and guide them.
- Creative people are naturally rebellious, and this inherently puts strain on their relationships with those who employ them.

4

The Diversity of Creativity

Little research has yet been undertaken into defining the different types of creativity – but then, as we have seen, little research has been undertaken into the nature of creativity at all. The wider problems have proved so daunting that researchers have been unwilling to complicate matters still further by attempting to sub-divide a concept itself as impenetrable as a Schoenberg symphony. On the contrary, most theorists have sought to simplify matters by claiming (or at least implying) that creativity is a unique, quantifiable entity – like gravity or oxygen – which will one day be identified and understood.

To some extent, as has been said, this book itself represents an attempt to unify the different forms of creativity. But the unification must not be permitted to distort the reality. To offer an analogy: all ball players share certain aptitudes, and most good ball players can turn their hands, or feet, to any ball-based sport. But cricketers are manifestly different from soccer players and both are different from tennis players, and so on. And soccer players themselves have a wide diversity of specialist skills (strikers and defenders are far from interchangeable, though both may be brilliant ball players) – as do cricketers and tennis players and all the others. The differences between the sports themselves are akin to the macro-differences between the creative arts – the differences between players of the same game are akin to the micro-differences.

Let's first deal with the micro-differences. As in sport, the principle differences between creative people in the same game are of three kinds: quality, style and technique.

First, quality. At the lowest common denominator, it is possible to argue that every single act that every single person in the world ever performs is creative: no other person has before done that particular thing at that particular time in that particular place in that particular way. ('Can I have the same again?' asks the customer in the old pub joke. 'Certainly not,' replies the witty barman, 'you can never have the same again, you can only have something similar'.)

A less rigorous and more common version of this argument runs: 'Everyone is creative, in their own way'. No contest. Even chimpanzees are creative, in their own way. Faced with the problem of retrieving a banana from a high shelf, a chimpanzee will build an ingenious (for a chimpanzee) assemblage of chairs, tables and sticks adequate to the task. So – ignoring chimpanzees – you can certainly define all human beings and all human acts as creative; but in that case you will need to find a new word to differentiate tinkling a pub piano from a Beethoven piano concerto.

That is a *reductio ad absurdum* of the argument that everybody and every act is creative – in its own way. There are manifestly differences between various qualities of creativity. As Chris Jones said, it is like running or jumping. Some people are amazingly good at running and jumping, some amazingly bad, and between the extremes there is a continuum. Scattered along the continuum (some of them closer to tinkling a piano in a pub, some of them closer to composing a concerto), are to be found building a garden shed and building Chartres cathedral, writing memos and writing *Crime and Punishment*, yodelling in the bath and singing *Carmen* at La Scala, doodling and painting *The Haywain* – all of which might be thought by their progenitors and practitioners to be creative.

Focusing more sharply on commercial creativity, also along the continuum you will find the novels of Barbara Cartland and of Leo Tolstoy, blocks of dreary council flats and the Sydney Opera House, home videos and *Citizen Kane*, lavatory cleaner commercials and the 'Heineken refreshes the parts other beers cannot reach' campaign. Once again all of them would probably – and rightly, if you accept the above definition of creativity – be claimed by their creators to be creative. But they are not all of the same quality.

For every project the creative manager will need to recognise and to determine the quality of the creativity which is appropriate. Simplistic textbooks usually claim that the manager should always aim for the best. That is codswallop. In all business transactions managers have to judge what quality is required, and what can be afforded. This is as true in the purchase of creativity as in the purchase of raw materials. The manager must indubitably always go for the best possible quality at the price. But no manager could afford to provide every member of a sales force with a Ferrari. Value, rather than quality alone, must be the transcendant evaluator.

In creativity, as everywhere, you generally get what you pay for – the higher the quality, the higher the price. As we have seen, the markets for creativity are uncommonly free and competitive; prices adjust to supply and demand with great rapidity and precision. Creative quality is always in short supply and in great demand. So that one of the principle functions of the creative manager is to decide upon the level of quality necessary, justifiable and affordable. This is an essential aspect of cost control, to which we shall return in Chapter 8.

The manager's difficulties are compounded by the fact that the quality of creative peoples' work – unlike the quality of most raw materials – is not only patchy, it is indefinable and immeasurable. This is as true of great artists as it is of more commonplace creators.

The creative manager must forever be alert to creators' mutations. Probably no creative industry suffers more from creative peoples' vagaries than the film industry. Steven Bach, in *Final Cut*, his marvellous case history of calamitous creative mismanagement, records how almost every great Hollywood talent – from Griffith to Gable, from Chaplin to Coppola, from Welles to Wilder – has on occasion (and usually on many occasions) produced box office flops. In every creative industry, but perhaps especially in the movies, the difficulties of inconsistency are aggravated by creators' egotism. And the bigger they are, the harder they fall. There will never be a watertight solution to this problem, but that does not provide the creative manager with a watertight excuse for ignoring it. It is one of many reasons why the creative manager must never be intimidated by – though he may well be, and probably should be, in awe of – the creative people with whom he is working.

The second area of creative micro-diversity – equally difficult to pinpoint precisely – is style. In the pure arts, creators of similar stature may be differentiated from each other in a host of ways: classic versus romantic, traditionalist versus radical, spiritual versus materialistic and so on. These are not differences of quality, but of attitude, vision and style. Such differences are at least as important in the world of commercial creativity. To the creative manager, they are a minefield. All good creators' have their own style. So do most creative businesses. When the two are mismatched havoc ensues – aggravated by the fact that it often takes a while for the problem to be identified, as differences in style are frequently far from obvious.

Few creative people are even aware of their own style. To them their style comes naturally and seems the right way, possibly the only way, to do things. Hence they are often unaware of its limitations. Consequently they seek jobs which they cannot do, or anyway cannot do well. Square pegs will have no idea that they are trying to force themselves into round holes, as likely as not they will be fascinated by the challenge. The effective manager must assess the varying creative styles of those with whom he is involved, and also know how far their styles can be stretched. Occasionally, perhaps on a small or unimportant job, the manager will take a calculated risk, and encourage a creator to try his hand at something that may be outside his range. Most of the time, however, it is the manager's job to pick the right style of horse for the right style of course, based on track record and proven abilities. There are more than enough risks in the management of creativity, without taking on unnecessary ones.

Moreover, differently from quality, there is unlikely to be any significant saving of money when the manager takes a risk on style. Creators may cut their fees a bit when trying something stylistically new (for them). But more often they will still go for their standard rate, because they are confident they can handle the new task (regardless of whether or not they can).

From questions of quality and style, let us turn to the third important area where kinds of creativity vary – differences of technique. The most common difference of technique manifests itself in differences between idea and execution. To develop the previous discussion, there are creative people who overflow with ideas but have little ability to execute them well and creative people who have fewer ideas but are wonderful craftsmen.

In every creative business there are borderlines, between the origination of ideas and their execution. Both can be equally creative (or uncreative, for that matter). The magazine editor is not necessarily more, or less, creative than the feature writer; the advertising art director is not necessarily more, or less, creative than the photographer he uses. Note that we are not here making any value judgment about the differences between creator and interpreter – that is, between composer and musician, or between author and actor, or writer and editor. All of them may be highly creative people, and there is often a surprising equivalence of salaries between them. Nor should it be thought, though it often is, that having ideas is creatively superior to executing them. As has previously been said, few great artists are renowned principally for their inventiveness.

Because they fail to recognise the equal importance of all phases in the creative process, many managers destroy good creative work by stinting on the resources they devote to the executional phase. This is dumb. The public, the customers, are frequently unable to differentiate between an idea and its execution. Even professional critics can rarely differentiate between an idea and its execution. If a basically poor idea is sufficiently well executed it will often achieve commercial success. Poor scripts brilliantly directed, poor commercials brilliantly produced, poor magazine articles brilliantly designed and illustrated – in each case the artifice may so enhance the original idea as to make it seem far better than it really is. The converse is rarely true. That is why it is perilous to penny-pinch at the executional stage of a creative project, and managers who do so court disaster.

Another problem managers frequently face, at the border between idea and execution, emanates from creative people who try to do too much. Many, if not most, creative people get bored with doing what they can do well and try to tackle things they do badly. It is the manager's tricky job to dissuade them. This is similar to the problem of creative people who try to work in too many styles.

In the creative industries specialisation of labour applies with a vengeance. Most creators, though they may not realise it, have a narrow range of creative abilities. Feature writers rarely make good fiction writers; designers are quite different from illustrators; fashion photographers can't shoot portraits; still photographers can't shoot movies; in advertising few creators of press advertising are really good at television commercials. I happen to be chairman of a television post production company where one of my partners is an outstanding editor of comedy programmes. At a pinch he can edit anything – but he has an instinct for the timing of hilarious sequences. Very few people can edit comedy as well as he does, and he does not aspire to edit other types of material. That's true specialisation. And in the creative industries, in one form or another, it is commonplace.

There are exceptions, but they are so infrequent as to be noteworthy. Some of the most massively talented creative people – Sir Lawrence Olivier and Orson Welles spring to mind – have been able to master a wide range of disparate creative roles. Such multi-facetted talents are few and far between. The creative manager should almost always urge creators to keep to their last, and to excel at the things they do well, rather than allow them to try and be jacks-of-all-trades.

Having discussed the diversity of creative talents – the micro-differences – we must now focus on the diversity of creative projects, the macro-differences.

The varying ways in which the creative industries are structured predictably results in a diversity of different problems arising for the managers within each of them. The key differences, from industry to industry, result from two factors. First, the cost and number of individual, separate, creative projects the organisation handles. Second, the degree of day-to-day interaction between the managers and the creators. The first is of far greater importance than the second, and experience suggests that it is hardly understood at all – either by creative people or by managers, and least of all by governments, when they get themselves involved with the creative industries, as they now so often do.

Put simply, it costs comparatively little to produce a new book whereas it costs a small fortune to produce a new movie; new gramophone records can be, and are, launched on shoestring budgets whereas new West End musicals can and frequently do turn multi-millionaires into paupers overnight; small advertising leaflets can be printed for a pittance whereas most television campaigns cost millions of pounds. These cost-per-project variations are of paramount importance, and the consequences that flow from them permeate many aspects of the management of creativity.

I have hammered home with the delicacy of a pile driver the message that commercial creativity inevitably involves a high degree of uncertainty and of financial risk. But for most book publishers, or record companies, the costs-per-project, and the commensurate financial risks, will be comparatively small. That is why publishers and record companies market so many titles and tunes. They spread their risks widely, knowing that many of their projects will fail, and hoping enough will come good to bear the cost of the failures. Any organisation marketing a vast number of new products cannot, however, afford to devote too much in the way of resources to any of them; not too much management time, not too much advertising or sales promotion, not too much quality control and little or no market research. Most of the individual projects do not warrant the time, and cannot carry the costs. Paul Hamlyn entertainingly says:

> As a publisher you get a lot of 'My dear Paul, my wife has written a book on Mongolian cooking. I'm sure you can cope with it.' I suppose I get a couple of dozen like that a week. So you become adept at saying 'No'. That is part of your skill. I have done it a couple of thousand times, I'm sure. And as a result one throws something good out mistakenly in some cases. Every publisher has lots of such stories. Here we're so big it would be impossible to watch everything. And it's not really my role. I'm a great believer in backing people up. But there are so many little pieces of the jigsaw, so many titles, so many authors, so many concepts, it's often very difficult.

Similar in certain respects to books and records are newspapers and weekly magazines. The production costs of each issue, *in toto*, are considerable but the effective cost per item will mostly be small. Because each issue comes, goes and rapidly turns into fish-and-chip wrapping there is a limit to the amount of time and attention which can be applied to everything within it. However, because magazines and newspapers enjoy 'brand loyalty' – which publishing houses and record companies have never achieved, to any degree – it may be worthwhile investing in the 'title', the implicit assumption being that the publication's format, and the consistency of its editorial control, will ensure that people who like one issue will also like the next, and the next. (A doctoral thesis needs to be written on the similarities and differences between branded publications and branded consumer goods.)

Likewise popular fashion goods share certain similarities with books and records. They are produced in astonishing variety, enjoy a comparatively short sales life, and therefore cannot support heavy investment costs per garment. A massive number of quick, instinctive decisions have to be taken by the creators and managers within the fashion industry, based on their judgment and experience, without the benefit of elaborate preparation or analysis.

At the other end of the spectrum is the blockbuster movie. In 1987 it cost $28.4 million to make, release and market the average Hollywood feature. A decade later in 1997 it cost $75.6 million. That's an average increase of over 10% annually, well ahead of the rate of inflation. (Incidentally confirming the thesis of Princeton's William Bowen that creative costs always tend to outpace general inflation). Moreover very nearly all that money is spent before a single ticket is sold. With so much dosh at stake comparatively few major films are made, and each gets star treatment from its makers. Only about 300 feature films are now produced each year in Britain and the US combined, compared with some 200,000 new books. While the creators working in most business sectors will be expected to produce many different 'products' in a year, often working on several at the same time, in feature films it is not uncommon to spend years working on a single project. The costs and the potential rewards justify it.

In consequence, every tiny aspect of a major film will be pored over and perused, questioned and qualified, dismembered and dissected, broken down and totted up by a plethora of executives all employed to minimise the possibility of failure. Despite all their care they fail with remarkable regularity. (It is estimated that far fewer than 50% of all feature films made ever reach the big silver screen.) Inevitably, the huge costs and concomitant risks force managers to try to play safe, to search desperately for proven creative formulae and lean heavily on market research.

These management disciplines could hardly be more different from those in the low cost-per-project creative industries like book publishing. Not that every book is cheap to produce, nor every film wildly expensive, but even extraordinarily expensive books cost only a fraction of the price of a major movie. As David Puttnam said in a *Time* magazine profile back in May 1989, shortly after he left Hollywood:

> As I learned to my cost at Columbia, almost every time you come up to it you're making a $20 million, or $30 million, or $50 million bet. That's not an environment that encourages risk or adventurous creative decisions.

The television industry deploys a wide range of both low-cost and high-cost programmes, and a corresponding variety of management styles. In Britain the smaller television companies operate more like book publishers than like film companies. They make a large number of programmes without too much fuss, allowing the creators relatively free rein. Here is Jeremy Isaacs describing how he ran Channel 4:

> They (the creative people) had to persuade me that their vision of the world was one that was worth backing. I didn't have to agree with it to back it. Indeed, it would be impertinent for the manager of an organisation that broadcasts or produces a lot of material to seek to identify himself or herself with every aspect of it. I think that is an arrogant line for a manager to take. Even if I did think something was wrong, if they could persuade me that they were right then they were certainly allowed to go ahead.

And here is Michael Grade on the same subject:

> My real job is to recognise the ideas that are dogs. That's basically what I do. I don't know for sure if something new is going to be successful, and if it is successful I have no way of knowing how successful it's going to be. I am really here to stop the ghastly ideas getting through. But I'm very persuadable. I look for obsession. I look for commitment. I look for them having thought the idea through. I want to be sure they understand any weaknesses in the idea. Then, if they still passionately want to do it, fine.

Jeremy Isaacs contrasts this with American television, where the stakes are much higher, and management controls far tighter:

> If you compare British television with American television you are comparing, in the first instance, a system in which a very great deal of respect is paid to the creator's wishes and intentions. You do not attempt to force the writers and directors into a strait-jacket: 'It's got to be like that otherwise we're not interested'. On the contrary you say: 'Hm, that's interesting, let's have a go. It ought to get quite a decent audience because it's on a really strong subject.' In America, exactly the opposite philosophy prevails: 'Our examination of your project tells us that it's got an unhappy ending, and that means it's not going to get a big audience, and so irrespective of how much I admire the script, I have to tell you we can't do this.' I once had an American executive tell me that what I was talking to him about was 'too good'. Such people are lobotomised, they're not using part of their minds. The result is a different sort of television. For the most part individuality, inspiration and creativity are mercilessly stamped out. It is in effect an industrial product, in which other considerations take priority over the creative instincts of the makers.

Sadly perhaps, the Isaacs/Grade approach to television programme commissioning is dwindling in prominence, even in Britain, and the major broadcasters (BBC1 and ITV3) are behaving increasingly like American broadcasters and movie makers. Programme ideas are picked over, submitted to committees, market researched, and endlessly revised and reworked. That is a corollary of the cost of producing expensive programmes that will gain mass audiences – and the perilous risks of failure. The smaller broadcasters, like BBC2 and Channel 4, can and do still make programme decisions on the basis of hunch and judgment. Independent production companies put forward proposals to commissioning editors over lunch, get a provisional 'yea' or 'nay', and press forward. The commissioning editors certainly won't give a conclusive decision at that stage, and they will invariably subject the project to further detailed scrutiny, but their initial response will be a good guide to the final outcome.

Thus the management systems which result from cost-per-project variances impinge heavily upon manager/creative relationships. This goes far to explain why creative people in many sectors enjoy much greater freedom in Britain than in America – it's a smaller market, with smaller costs, and smaller risks. It perhaps equally explains, as a direct consequence, why the creative industries appear to flourish more abundantly here than in the United States. To quote from Sir Denis Forman's celebrated 1984 MacTaggart lecture:

In the matter of entertainment and the performing arts, we are top dogs. British theatre, British television, British films have built a respect for British values which has an incalculable effect upon the psychology of the transatlantic relationship. It is the last field of world leadership left open to us, and we neglect it at our peril.

That may bang our drum a little too loudly. The balance between management power and creative power is a delicate one. Nonetheless Forman reflects the truth that in American creative industries the management often exercises its authority a trifle too ham-fistedly, and many of the results are neither attractive creatively nor that successful commercially. However, the difficulties involved in handling expensive, high-risk creativity are by no means simple to resolve, as Jeremy Isaacs explains:

One of the reasons why a lot of people who make huge successes of managing commercial television then make idiots of themselves in the film industry, is that the elements of safety and risk are so totally different in each case. In British television it has simply been impossible to spend more on wrong creative decisions than any ITV company could earn from advertising revenue. So there was a huge degree of freedom within which to take chances. They then went to the cinema where it's all risk and no guarantee. Wrong decisions there, and it's disaster.

The disaster is exacerbated by the fact that on television the multiplicity of programmes means that the occasional fiasco will soon be lost and forgotten, whereas movies often sink to a fanfare of trumpets. Creative people however are not concerned with such differences. They simply want to get their work produced, unimpeded and unhindered by management.

Another corollary of size is that creative projects involving hundreds of millions of pounds (blockbuster movies, public buildings) will involve hundreds and maybe thousands of creative people. While creativity is inherently an individual process, large projects inevitably mean teamwork. Teamwork is not a way of working which many creative people find salubrious – unless they are in control of the team. They aren't natural teamplayers. Independence is, as we saw in the last chapter, a basic personality trait. (It is the *corps de ballet* problem again.)

Wally Olins here summarises both the need for teamwork and some of the problems it inevitably entails:

We do huge, incredibly complex jobs. Nobody can do them alone, it's just not possible, there's just too much to do. One person can inspire the team, but one person can't do everything. The disciplines that are involved are very complex, and they're inter-related. There are project managers who look after the totality; there are graphic designers at various levels of seniority; there are architectural designers; there are print designers; there are typographical designers, and communications experts, and so on and so forth. Many of these people have little respect for the others. There are many aspects of a creative business where people don't respect each other's talents. They think the others get away with things, they think they're no bloody good, they think they let us all down – there's a lot of that. People within the organisation think that some people are too precious, they take too long, they make too much of a meal of it, they think they're too bloody brilliant – all that kind of stuff. However, here they have to work in teams. They haven't any alternative. And usually when they work in teams even the most selfish of them, in the end, begins to recognise that they couldn't work outside a team. And if they antagonise the other members of the team they find themselves in a worse position. So they begin to work better.

The dynamics of social interaction in small groups, when people work together on related tasks, have been well-researched and documented.

Most of the studies have been carried out among general, non-creative groups, but Wally Olins' easily recognisable description of the process shows that in this respect at least, creators' behaviour is far from atypical.

Interestingly, and perhaps surprisingly, this spotlights one area of creative diversity that might have been expected to lead to a host of differing management problems but does not appear to do so. Because creative people in the different arts and disciplines, the macro-sectors – music, writing, design and so on – share similar personality traits, they require similar styles of management. Wally Olins expresses the position thus:

> I have quite a lot to do with writers, and quite a lot to do with architects, and with creative people in what you might call the graphic trades, and I don't see a vast difference between them emotionally.

He goes on to say that because of their training, and because of the very different job functions they perform, there are sometimes intellectual differences between, eg, architects and illustrators. David Puttnam feels that such differences as there are lie between originators (composers) and interpreters (instrumentalists). But, again, he does not generally feel the differences to be fundamental.

The last important area where macro-sector, industry-to-industry variations influence management/creative relationships results from the different levels of day-to-day contact. To take the extremes once again: having commissioned a book the publisher may have no further contact with the author for months or even years, whereas a film producer and his director will work together daily (and often nightly) throughout the duration of the production.

Inevitably, the closeness or distance of such relationships will effect the personal interactions between manager and creator, and will effect the ways in which they influence each other. To illustrate this point, consider the opinions of Christopher Bland, Michael Grade and Paul Hamlyn, quoted in Chapter 3, on the question of whether it is necessary for managers to like the creative people they deal with. They all say it isn't. But then none of them has to work in close proximity with individual creative people on a day-to-day basis for protracted periods. David Puttnam who, like any film producer, will find himself living and working cheek-by-jowl with the same creators day and night, week after week, month after month, is far less sanguine about the problem:

Working with people I dislike, even talented people, would destroy the atmosphere of teamwork, which is half of the pleasure of being in a creative business. I've had chunks of my life made miserable by other people's egos. I doubt if I'd work with them now. I don't think it's worth it.

Frequency of contact not only effects personal relationships, it also effects the processes of briefing, amendment and rejection, to which we will return in Chapter 9. It is also, again, the consequence of cost-per-project variations: the publisher cannot afford to spend much time with each of his authors, whereas the film producer needs to keep a tight grip on the project from beginning to end. Thus, there is much diversity, both of creativity itself and of the relationships in the industries within which it flourishes.

In this and the preceding chapters we have concentrated on creativity, though the managers have reared their usually unpopular heads from time-to-time, like interlopers. It is now time to focus more tightly on the managers' role in this labyrinthine jungle.

SUMMARY

- Although it is possible to consider commercial creativity as an entirety, this must not be permitted to blur the considerable variations that exist.
- There are micro-variations between creative people in each commercial sector; these are principally differences of quality, style and technique.
- Differences of quality are almost always reflected in price; differences in style are not, usually, nor are differences in technique.
- Few creative people have as much diversity of talent as they think they have, and the manager should almost always encourage them to stick to their lasts.
- There are macro-differences between the various creative sectors, principally based on the costs involved in individual projects.
- From such cost differences flow a variety of consequences, particularly the time and resources that can be devoted to each of them, and the level of risk that can be taken.
- These differences also impinge on the personal day-to-day involvement between managers and creators, and bigger projects inevitably tend to aggravate latent personal discord more than smaller ones.

5

The Role of the Manager

'*Management is, all things considered, the most creative of all arts. It is the art of art. Because it is the organiser of talent*,' says the eminent French thinker, Jean-Jacques Servan-Schreiber, in a neat fusion of the twin themes of this book.

Not everyone would put management on quite so high a pedestal. Least of all those creative people who tend to feel that the executives whose job it is to manage them are at best worthy, and often as not utterly incompetent. While David Puttnam, at the top of the ladder, believes it to be vital for managers and creators to respect each others abilities, lower down the rungs the relationships between managers and creators are often hostile, suspicious and mutually disparaging. All of which results, in some measure, from managers' lack of understanding of exactly what their role should be. But about this there really should not be any doubt. '*Your prime role as a manager*,' says Jeremy Isaacs, '*is enabling creativity to fulfil itself. That's what you're there to do. You're not there to stop people being creative, you're there to help people be creative.*'

As a succinct statement of the creative manager's job, that can hardly be bettered. Isaacs is fond of the concept of the manager as 'enabler'. Michael Grade uses an orchestral analogy, describing the manager as '*a conductor, with a lot of soloists*'. David Puttnam prefers the word 'facilitator', which is almost a synonym of 'enabler'. He emphasises that the facilitator must never become, or be seen to be, a 'servant' of the creators:

> The manager is a facilitator, and I don't think the facilitator is a servant, but someone who makes things possible. If the manager sees himself as a servant – which is what happened to film producers in France, in the Sixties and Seventies – the whole damn thing goes down the sink eventually, because the film maker doesn't want a servant. He wants a colleague.

For the colleague to carry out his enabling role effectively, he must fulfil five basic functions. He must recruit the right creators for the job; provide the right ambience; motivate them to excel; ensure they deliver at the right time and at the right cost; and get them to create the right creative product. We shall be exploring each of these functions in turn. In aggregate, the role they define – the creative manager's role – is palpably a demanding one.

There are not that many individuals for whom the management of creative people is their full-time job. For most, it is only a part of their job, though often an exceedingly important part. Perhaps that is why so little attention has been paid to the management of creativity in the past. The job titles of those involved vary from industry to industry; publisher, producer, controller, account executive, project manager, creative manager, planner (or any combination of these or similar words). Within the creative industries they all denote jobs which imply a close supervisory involvement with the creators.

Other management functions, not quite so close to the creative coalface, may also involve frequent interaction with creative people; chief executives and managing directors, production directors, marketing and brand managers, managing editors, programme controllers, co-ordinators, sales management and even personnel. As creativity percolates into more and more aspects of business a host of managers, with all kinds of functions and titles, sporadically find themselves dealing with creative people on occasional jobs and projects.

A minority of those whose principal job is creative management themselves begin their careers as creators, but decide at some stage that they prefer management to creativity. (Or maybe their superiors make the decision for them!) I myself started out as an advertising copywriter, but rapidly decided I wasn't much cop at it and would be better at managing than doing. Having once worked as a creator has obvious advantages. It helps the manager to see the issues from both sides of the fence. As Jeremy Isaacs states:

> I have the insight of having been somebody himself who, by trying to make programmes as well as he possibly could, had to fight for the conditions in which it was possible to make them. I found out from being that side of the fence to what extent one had to live efficiently within whatever constraints were necessary, and to what extent one was sometimes entitled to say to the boss, 'I've got to have a bit more room here.'

Often the heads of creative departments will still be practising creators, dividing their time, uncomfortably, between producing their own creative work and running their department. Trying to keep both balls in the air often gives them an awkward squint; they rarely do either job consummately well. Such individuals usually find it intensely difficult to settle down into full-time management roles. It is as though they had become addicted to creativity – addiction being the appropriate word, since they patently suffer withdrawal symptoms when they try to kick the creative habit.

It is fascinating, in passing, to note that the addictive power of creativity is not just a human phenomenon, but is a more basic animal instinct. In his book, *The Biology of Art*, Desmond Morris writes:

> Apes, both young and adult, can become engrossed in picture-making to the point where they prefer it to being fed and will exhibit temper tantrums if they are stopped.

Perhaps it is fortunate, then, that the majority of creative managers have never tried their hands at being creative, and are modest about their own creative talents. To quote Chris Jones again:

> You have to realise in your heart of hearts that you can't do what they do.
> It comes with a recognition they have something you don't.

Indeed, many managers in creatively based industries do not regard themselves or their jobs as creative and are uncomfortable with creative people, according to Stanley S Gryskiewicz, director of Creativity Development at the Centre for Creative Leadership in America. This, as we shall see in Chapter 11, has advantages as well as disadvantages as it enhances the excitement and pleasure that they get from working with creators. But if managers have not worked closely with professional creators early in their careers it is exceptionally rare for them to become good at it later in life.

Managers who have been brought up on a strict diet of production controllers, systems analysts, supplies officers, finance directors and the like – that is, managers who have spent their working lives dealing with other managers – invariably choke on the indigestible ways of full-time creators if they first come across them half-way through their careers. This is the source of a disastrous mistake often made by the headquarters of conglomerates and other large organisations when one of their 'creative subsidiaries' goes awry. The HQ honchos draft in a senior manager, with little or no experience of commercial creativity, to put things right. Everybody is then bewildered when everything goes wrong. Steven Bach's *Final Cut* painfully demonstrates how poorly Transamerica Insurance understood the operations of its United Artists film-making subsidiary, hard as it tried. When UA ran into trouble, Transamerica appointed an intelligent, thoughtful, hard-working, conscientious and well-intentioned businessman to run it – a splendid chap in many respects, but with no knowledge of the movie business. Two years later United Artists collapsed.

One of the cardinal reasons why experienced novices cannot be expected to handle the role of creative manager successfully is that they cannot master the first of the essential management functions; the recruitment of the right creators. This is not an ability that can be acquired overnight, nor can it be rapidly absorbed on a management training course. To be good at it the manager must both enjoy and be perceptive about creativity, in all its many facets. (Most of those who meet both criteria will have sought employment in the creative industry of their choice early on in life.) The manager must be able to recognise and put the appropriate value on creative quality, style and technique. A newcomer, no matter how intelligent, thoughtful, hard-working, conscientious, well-intentioned and splendid does not have a cat in hell's hope of succeeding. To some extent the job can delegated. That is what casting directors do in movies, television and live theatre. But the top manager must still be the final arbiter. To delegate completely the power of recruitment is to delegate control of the creative product. To reprise Jeremy Isaacs:

> In inviting them to do the job you've made your creative decision, which is which creator to work with.

How does the creative manager reach those basic decisions, the recognition and employment of the right talented people? Without the right people the rest of the creative edifice can never be built. Creativity can be nurtured and developed – but unlike kidneys and teeth it cannot be implanted. This is a direct corollary of the argument advanced in the last chapter. If creativity were something that people had or did not have – like ten fingers or brown eyes – then it would be easy to divide the haves from the have-nots. But because creativity is not like that the manager needs to be able to discern fine differences, the differences of creative quality, style and technique. Every designer, musician or writer applying for a job is likely to be quite good, but which will be right? (When, on one occasion, I questioned the first part of the thesis, I was sharply corrected by a head-hunter, who said: 'Nobody thinks they can design, or sing, or write, if they can't do it at all. The people who apply for such jobs always have some aptitude. The eternal problem is; how much, and what is it like?')

How do managers identify the right people for the right jobs? We have seen that intelligence is a far from perfect guide. Worse, it is often positively misleading. People who are intelligent are usually articulate, confident and perform well in interviews. As a result, managers tend to react warmly to them, and reject inarticulate interviewees who may be much more talented. When recruiting creators, verbal responses during the interview must not be overrated. (And to avoid doing so can be exceptionally difficult, as we all tend to like, and rate highly, people we can talk to.) The interviewer must keep in mind not only the comparative irrelevance of high intelligence, but also the personality traits associated with creativity. The best applicant may well display insecurity, rebelliousness, stubbornness and egotism – none of which are likely to enhance his interview performance. Hence, personal interviews – never wholly reliable as a means of assessing people's abilities – are especially unreliable in the case of creators.

Nevertheless there are things managers can do to maximise their success rate. You must be sure to keep in mind creative people's insecurities; be particularly attentive and sensitive to the individual; minimise interruptions; don't take telephone calls; don't rummage through your desk drawers; don't fiddle with your computer and don't open the post. Give all interviewees the impression that for 15 or 20 minutes they are the most important people in the world. Some managers think it's smart to be calculatedly aggressive, to put respondents on their mettle, to run interviews as though they were pugilistic bouts. That may or may not be helpful in the recruitment of tough negotiators or sales representatives. In the recruitment of creators it is almost guaranteed to be catastrophic.

New York University's Bernard Weiss lists the following common pitfalls to avoid during interviews with creative people:

- Taking notes when the candidate is revealing sensitive, potentially damaging or personal information. Wait for a change in the topic, or until the applicant is discussing something favourable or positive, before taking notes.

- Asking questions likely to be answered with a curt 'yes' or 'no' – and that's it. With less verbal people you need a list of leading questions, such as 'What things are prompting you to consider leaving your present job?' or 'What five things have you done that you are most proud of?'

- Conducting an inquisition. Although the interview is being conducted at your request, your guest should feel involved in a discussion, not a courtroom investigation.

Creative tests, of which there are many, are useful for establishing whether otherwise ordinary people do or do not have any creative spark, but are no help whatsoever in assessing the degree of talent in reasonably (or highly) creative individuals. Tests which measure an awareness of good design have been shown to be the most powerful tests yet discovered as a predictor of creative potential in any field of endeavour. In other words creative writers, musicians and artists of all kinds almost universally have an eye for good design. But once again such tests cannot identify fine differences of quality, let alone differences in style or technique.

In any event it is rarely possible to get senior creative people to take creativity tests. It is like getting top actors to attend casting sessions. Fortunately this matters little, since studies have consistently shown that the most reliable way to identify an individual's future creative performance is through his previous creative performance. The best way to tell if he will do well in future is to examine what he has done in the past. In assessing past performance the manager is greatly aided by creators' predilection for fame. As creators are personally identified with their work, it is comparatively easy for the manager to spot and keep methodical track of talented people. Anyway, managers need to track precisely who is producing what in order to keep fully abreast of current trends and fashions. In my experience good managers of creativity always know exactly who in their industry has done what, and when, and working with whom. Such knowledge is their stock in trade; without it they could not do their jobs. (And that information, too is truly difficult for a newcomer to an industry to acquire. Even computers aren't much help.)

Unfortunately, no rules can be defined which will readily tell a manager how to spot talent. That seems itself to be an inborn talent, as leading creative managers recognise:

> I'm not terribly creative myself, but I do think I'm good at spotting creative people. I don't think there is any real training for it. It's the nose, the hunch. I'm a great believer in that. And if you have the nose, all in all you get it right.
>
> (Paul Hamlyn)

> I think that I have a creative instinct. I think that I have an inner eye.
>
> (Wally Olins)

Nose, eye, instinct or hunch can all be honed and sharpened with experience. For example, cynical though it may sound, it pays to be suspicious. Individuals' output may be branded with their names, but that by no means proves it is all their own work. Success has many parents and creators are as prone to plagiarise, fib and exaggerate their contribution to anything that has succeeded as the rest of humanity (if not more so). On two separate occasions dumb and idle creative blokes have presented me with award-winning advertisements which they claimed as their own but which had been produced years earlier in my agency. Moreover, creators frequently work well within a particular team or ambience, but fail as soon as they venture outside. They themselves may genuinely not appreciate their dependence on a set of colleagues, the manager must. To quote Chris Jones:

> Creative people may flourish in one environment and you transfer them to another apparently similar environment and they fail. Nobody knows why.

One of the most common management pitfalls is the failure to spot the transitory effect upon an inferior talent of working within a brilliant team. Just as in any sport, everyone plays better alongside better players. The dilemma for the manager is to decide exactly how much (or how little) of the superior talent has been absorbed, and to what extent the prospective employee has been permanently improved by the association. Thus, some average cameramen shoot marvellously when inspired by great directors, but are lost when left to themselves. Others learn from the directors, and go on to become fine directors in their own right.

Having spotted the talent, the next hurdle is to recruit it. (In most creative businesses this may be outside the control of any but the most senior management.) Good creative people are always in demand, and know they are. So for them job selection is a two-way process. To some degree this is always the case with good people; with good creative people the degree is much greater than average. They will be just as anxious as their prospective employer to ensure that the job is right for them. Many a manager has emerged from interviewing a creator wondering dazedly who was choosing whom. Though no statistics exist, it is a safe bet that creative people are more prone than others to reject job offers – even after lengthy and detailed negotiations. Their main asset being their talent they must ensure that asset is invested to their maximum advantage.

Many of the factors which influence a creator's job choices will be the same as would influence anyone else. However, two factors hold particular significance for them, and managers should relegate even such a prime consideration as remuneration to third or fourth place. First, creators are always massively concerned about the reputation of any employer; and second, they are concerned whether the employer will provide them, personally, with opportunities to produce outstanding work. The two are interlocked, and both are embedded in the creative personality and its intricacies.

It is doubtful whether employees in any other type of industry spend as much time discussing the merits and demerits of the companies in their field. To outsiders, overhearing creative people in pubs and at parties, the intensity of their interest will sound veritably obsessive. They will debate endlessly whether architect S's star is rising while architect W is on the wane; whether advertising agency PJ&K is the current hotshop while QYM&Z has passed its peak; whether record company zeta has the newest sounds, while theta seems to be going MOR and beta hasn't had a cool group in years.

In *Final Cut*, Steven Bach relates how United Artists put a massive effort into improving its creative image, not with the public but within the movie business. It was because UA was scared of falling out with director Michael Cimino – then a hot creative property – that they allowed him to overspend grossly on *Heaven's Gate* and thus drive the company towards oblivion. Why were they so scared? Because if Cimino had quit it would have been detrimental to their reputation as creative movie-makers. Why did that matter? Because without a creative reputation the company would not be able to recruit top stars, top writers, top directors, top talent of any kind. It's the same in advertising, publishing, fashion, architecture … all creators want to work with the companies with the top creative reputations. They may well accept less money, and even lousy working conditions, to do so.

Nor are they altogether wrong. As has been noted, working with other top creators will burnish their talent. Even if it does so only temporarily, it will provide them with the opportunity to produce work which will enhance their reputation for the future. If it does so permanently, the value of their talent will be increased for good. Creators learn from other creators. 'Twas ever thus; that is what great artists' ateliers were about. Moreover the best companies get the best commissions, clients and projects, which helps them continue to produce the best work, which helps them to continue to recruit the best staff, and so they continue to get the best commissions. The system would be eternally self-perpetuating but for the fact that even the brightest creative stars eventually fade.

If a company does not have a strong creative reputation it will nonetheless need to convince talented prospective employees of its ability to provide them with the opportunity to produce outstanding work. The employee will be well aware that the organisation is not burgeoning with talent. In the unlikely event that the employee has not noticed he will have been told about it by creative friends, and will be concerned about the effect upon his own reputation of working for an organisation with a poor creative image. The employer may be able to turn this to advantage by pointing out to the potential recruit that here is a unique personal opportunity to improve the quality of the work, and thus to build the company's creative image. ('After all, if you're working at PJ&K you'll just be one fish in a crowded creative pond. While here at QYM&Z you'll have the pond all to yourself and any improvements will be seen to be your own.') Having made such a promise, the creative manager must work hard to make it come true. Talented creators are never short of job offers and competitors circle over unhappy ones like birds of prey inspecting a tasty morsel.

None of this should have come as a surprise. Creators' attitudes to their jobs, and thus to their employers, can be deduced from their personality traits. Because they are people who want to be judged by their output, the quality of their output matters intensely to them, and they recognise that this is in large measure dependent upon the quality of their employer. They are egotistical and insecure, both of which characteristics will be massaged if they work for organisations with high reputations. They are stubborn and rebellious, both of which will be better understood and accepted within creative, rather than uncreative, organisations. They are perfectionists, and so job satisfaction is of great importance to them. All of which makes them picky when choosing jobs.

Naturally their attitude to the job will vary if it does not involve full-time employment. Creators being employed on a freelance or project basis, to carry out an assignment which will not last too long, and may be covert, may well be less choosy. After all, the next job may be better, and anyway nobody need know they have worked on this one. But even in this situation creators will be well aware that carrying out too many hack jobs will harm their reputation, lower their value, and therefore their income, and won't be much fun anyway. The less good creators have little choice, they have to take what they can get. But, particularly when getting started, as has been mentioned, highly talented freelance creators often charge lower fees for the jobs they really want – providing managers who are on the ball with cost-saving bargains.

On the subject of employing freelancers and consultants, one last important point. In few other industries are lawyers busier, or happier, or remunerated more handsomely. In few other industries is there more litigation between employers and employee. In his sensational exposé of the seamier side of Hollywood, *Indecent Exposure*, author David McClintick writes: *'The entertainment industry functions in a jungle of contracts.'* The same is true of all the creative industries. (*'I've always hired the heaviest and hardest lawyers'*, admits Alan McGee.) Partly this results from the amorphous nature of creativity, which makes it so difficult to say whether or not the creators have really delivered the goods they promised; partly it is due to the complexities of copyright law; partly it is because creators' remunerations are often structured in complicated ways; partly it is because creators' innate rebelliousness makes them litigious; partly it is because creative managers frequently fail to tie up loose ends as tightly as they should. Whatever the reasons, there can be no doubt that one of the key responsibilities of every manager who employs creators – particularly on an *ad hoc* or project basis – is to draw up the most precise specification possible for each assignment. Lawyers and legal documentation are unavoidable, even though their powers to control creators are, finally, limited.

In the 1970s I ran a 'Poem of the Month Club'. I never expected it to be the most lucrative venture in the history of commerce, but it was good fun. Many of the world's finest and most celebrated poets contributed poems, including WH Auden, Sir John Betjeman, Cecil Day Lewis, Robert Graves, Thom Gunn, Seamus Heaney, Stevie Smith, Stephen Spender and a galaxy of others. From the start my partner warned that watertight contracts would have to be drawn up with each contributor because, he said, world famous poets were up to even more chicanery, and were even less reliable, than businessmen. He proved right. One of this century's finest poets – one named in the list – sold us a poem that had already been sold to somebody else, and which had been published abroad, which he hoped we would never discover. Nor did we, until one of our readers told us. The poet resolutely refused to return his fee. We would have been forced to go to court had we insisted on reclaiming it. He knew we would not.

For many managers of creativity the job of finding and recruiting creators will not be one of their responsibilities. It will be the responsibility of the head of the company, or the head of the department. They will be expected to work with the creators they are given, so to speak, and only be able to change them by making an inordinate fuss. And maybe not even then. Nor does the individual manager always have much control over the total ambience, the soil in which the creators are expected to flower – though every manager can and must ensure that the particular projects on which he is working are, within the existing ambience, as stimulating as can be.

While the buildings in which people work naturally influence them, and sometimes say a good deal about an organisation's attitudes to its employees, in my unfashionable view too much emphasis is often placed upon the physical ambience and too little on the personal ambience. The archetypal picture of the great creator working in an unsalubrious attic is not without validity. Most good creators have powerful concentration, and can immerse themselves in their thoughts, and in the job, almost oblivious of their surroundings. And many creators constantly move from place to place, pitching their tent wherever they have to. All creators want the relevant *facilities* to be perfect. Musicians are concerned about sound quality, artists about light, performers want to be heard, photographers require perfect equipment, designers nowadays need computers to hand, writers need silence and so on. But comfort and appearance, though not insignificant, are rarely crucial.

Obviously the nature of the physical environment will vary greatly from industry to industry. Films are shot on sets and on location; television programmes are made in studios and on location; writers work at home; musicians work in rehearsal rooms; photographers and journalists roam around and so on. Many small creative companies operate successfully from shambolic, over-crowded and dilapidated offices, and many creators seem to like it that way. Few journalists admit to liking their modern, hushed, computer-laden offices nearly as much as their old, crowded, Remington-clattering newsrooms. Here is Paul Hamlyn describing his company's move to the splendidly elegant Bibendum building, when it opened in South Kensington:

> I fought hard to get this building because I believe this is the sort of environment that creative people can work best in. But a lot of them hate it.

And Christopher Bland, on the same theme, says:

> Many great publishers and many great editors have worked in higgledy-piggledy offices stuffed with books and crowded with paper. Offices which have never seen the hand of a design consultant anywhere near them. Take Century Hutchinson. Hutchinson used to work in a thoroughly poky environment, but when Century Hutchinson joined together they moved into rather more spacious, open plan, modern, comfortable premises. I'm not sure that people are working necessarily either better or worse. It would be difficult to prove, either way.

Even Jeremy Myerson, a director at the Royal College of Art and a keen evangelist for 'creative office space' admits:

> The jury is still out on whether employees really feel more creative and productive working in them.

Despite such uncertainties, some creative organisations – particularly architectural and design consultancies – believe their physical and structural environment to be of the greatest importance. In the United

States, Scandinavia and the Netherlands many organisations have embraced 'hot desking' – where nobody has their own office, and people plonk themselves down wherever they can find space to plug in their laptops – confident that they encourage democratic thought, teamwork and a culture that is both creative and functional. Wally Olins believes this to be so for his company:

> The environment is key, the physical atmosphere in the building. We don't want a situation emerging where people are secretly working for days or weeks, nights or weekends, on a project which, when they present it, is quite clearly nonsensical ... The building is the key to the way we run the business. Everybody is accessible. The chairman's office is open plan, in the centre of the work-space. If I'm not in it and somebody wants to use it, they use it. This is done (a) because we want to be accessible, and (b) because we want to show people we have respect for them as human beings.

A few advertising agencies share Olins' convictions – particularly two young, fashionable and successful agencies called HHCL and St Luke's – but they are a minority. Most are concerned with the cosmetic appearance of their reception and their important conference rooms, but otherwise work in fairly conventional offices – like the majority of other creative businesses.

In the fashionable, Gadarene rush to encourage creativity, those few management theorists who have written about the subject appear to have forgotten that the role of the manager is not simply to keep the creators cheerful but, as Christopher Bland puts it, *'to create an environment in which creative people can enjoy themselves – without running riot'*. Jeremy Isaacs spells it out more fully:

> The problem of employing creative people in an organisation which in any sense is an industrial one is that their creativity sometimes needs to be tempered to the constraints within which the organisation is able to work ... they have to be creative within the budget that you can afford and on a timetable that enables you to plan.

In other words the manager's responsibilities are not solely, or even principally, to the creators. Having found the right creators for the job, the manager must ensure that they deliver a final product which is superior to that which they might have produced on their own, and – much more importantly, as we live in a competitive world – is superior to that which any other creative organisation would have produced.

As has already been stressed, the manager is the interface between creativity and other people. Usually the other people will be customers or clients, but they may also be colleagues within the organisation, or the public at large. To all these people the manager, and not the creators, will be the person responsible for delivering the creative product to them. So his role is not merely to butter-up the creators. If that were the job it would be laughably easy. But as Michael Grade states:

> As I keep reminding people here at Channel 4, ten times a week, it's the viewer who is sovereign, not the producer, not the head of department, not the commissioning editor, not me. We're all here to serve the audience, and nothing must get in the way of that.

To do so the ambience must allow the manager to question and criticise the work of the creators – however difficult that may be with creators who may be leaders in their field. Nor, if they are wise, will talented creators want to work in an ambience they can dominate. To quote David Puttnam:

> It is as important for the manager to respect the artist as for the artist to respect the manager. If either gets hopelessly out of kilter, lousy work is the result.

'How many times,' asks the writer Anne Billson, *'does one get the feeling, watching a film nowadays, that the director could have done with someone who might have given him a slap on the wrist, someone who might have said, "Hang on, this is what the public wants," someone with enough confidence in his own opinions and judgment to challenge the maestro at work?'*

The manager must encourage creators to excel with restraint; he must ensure they deliver excellence at the right time and at the right cost; and he must get them to create the ideal creative product for its market. We'll now take those apparently self-contradictory objectives one by one.

SUMMARY

- The prime job of the creative manager is to be an 'enabler', or 'facilitator'.
- Only a few creative managers start out as creators, and those that do often find it difficult to sort out their roles.

- Even fewer executives who move into creative management late in their careers ever become good at it.
- They particularly lack the vital experience and know-how to select the right creative people for each job.
- Good creative people are themselves exceedingly picky about their jobs.
- They are especially concerned about the creative reputations of prospective employers, and the opportunities they will get to produce outstanding work.
- Interviewing creative people demands particular care – and scepticism.
- Not everyone agrees about the importance of physical environment in improving creativity – but all good creative people demand top-class, relevant facilities.
- The manager must never forget, nor allow the creators to forget, that the work being created is for other people, for a market, not for themselves.

6

Motivating Creativity

Managing creativity is not unlike driving a car in town – bursts of acceleration, frequent braking, unforeseeable hazards, numerous changes of direction and a high risk of accident. Rarely is it like driving on a deserted motorway, demanding only attentiveness and a gentle nudge of the wheel from time to time. In this chapter we will be exploring the means of acceleration.

All good management involves leadership. The leadership of creative people is particularly difficult because they are prone to disdain leaders. They will admire tremendously, and may try to emulate, other creators. But managers, lacking overt creative talent, can find it hard to win their esteem. Outside of the creative industries, in the great mass of boss/subordinate relationships, subordinates accept instructions because they recognise that is how organisational hierarchies function, and they recognise that organisational hierarchies are an unavoidable fact of life. Few creators accept that organisational hierarchies are an unavoidable fact of life. If a manager is to lead them he must get their respect, and to get their respect he must earn it. It will not be bestowed upon him merely because of his status in the hierarchy.

Throughout history thinkers have debated whether leaders are born or made. Indubitably some individuals have a great deal of the characteristic called charisma. ('Charisma', a much misused word, literally means 'a gift from God'; something you are born with, not something that can be acquired.) Charismatic leaders, then, are born with some peculiar quality which makes people follow them. Whether or not charisma is a gift from God, it is not a unique quality which differentiates those who have it from those who do not. It is, like creativity itself, a quality which almost everybody has in some degree – like height and weight, or the ability to run and jump. So that almost everybody can unquestionably acquire basic leadership skills, just as quite average army officers can be taught to be highly effective leaders in battle.

Management guru Charles Handy, a visiting professor at the London Business School, provided a useful definition of the nature of managerial leadership in his book *The Age of Unreason*. '*A leader shapes and shares a vision which gives point to the work of others*' Handy says, and goes on to define five key aspects of successful leadership:

- The leader's vision must be different.
- The leader's vision must make sense to others.
- The leader's vision must be understandable.
- The leader must live the vision.
- The leader must remember that the vision will remain a dream without the work of others.

Charles Handy's general definition almost exactly matches Jeremy Isaacs' description of the role of the creative manager:

> The absolutely critical thing is that you have to make clear to them that you can offer them a vision of your intention in running the organisation which they can realise matches theirs, that you believe in what they believe in. It is not done by making great speeches. It is done by knowing what you want to do yourself, and being able to communicate it simply, directly and in a friendly manner. They don't have to feel you share their tastes. They have to feel that you have room in your pantheon for their own expression of their particular vision.

In order to motivate the work of others, especially when the others are creators, the leader must set them challenges, make them stretch themselves. As we have seen, new things rarely come into existence without a struggle. One of the paradoxes of creativity is that creators desperately want to create yet often have to be forced to do so. (This is not such uncommon human behaviour; many sportsmen desperately want to improve their performance yet still need tough trainers to bully them into it.) This is how David Puttnam sees it:

> Very good creative work falls into the area of problem solving. All you've got to do is to set the problem. You set the challenge, you set the objective, and the creative person can function within those parameters.

Alan McGee believes that making creators feel challenged, not to say threatened, is one of the most important weapons in the manager's armory:

> Sometimes to make great music it's not about being nice. I convince them everybody is against us. It's the band against the world. They feel their backs are up against the wall. Then I convince them we're going to fight this together. And we do.

Setting the challenge leads to the subject of briefing, which will be discussed fully in the next chapter. But there are other, equally important aspects of challenge; criticising poor work and the maintenance of high standards. Managers who approve all the creative work shown to them soon lose credibility and respect. All creators know their work is patchy, much as it galls them to acknowledge it. All creators know there are times when they need to be pushed, even if they will never admit it. It is something about which Puttnam feels especially keen:

> The demand for excellence is vital. For creative people competence is only acceptable as a point of departure, *en route* towards excellence or even greatness. Never allow competence to be an end result. The first idea they have is a point of departure, seldom an answer. The manager must not allow it to be an answer, because they might start to believe they're a genius. In addition, the manager must not allow emotional creativity to detract from the value of sheer professionalism. The manager must have a very definite and well-understood demand for professionalism, and not allow the notion of genius to detract from his day-to-day insistence on professionalism.

David Puttnam's empirical finding is confirmed by Professor William B Kirkwood, of East Tennessee State University:

> Research on how people solve tough, unfamiliar problems suggests that the first solution considered is rarely as original or as useful as the second or third. Why? The first idea that comes to mind will usually be the most obvious. Of course, if the problem we face is routine, this may be good enough. But if the task is difficult and unusual, obvious answers will not work. Unless we get past the obvious, we are unlikely to meet the challenge.

Tim Bell, agreeing with Anne Billson in the last chapter, believes that this is an area where managers of creative people are unacceptably lax:

> One thing that is wrong with the advertising business is that (managers) are frightened. So although a very large number of the ideas the creators come up with aren't any good, they don't have the guts to say 'that's rubbish'. So the creators get an easy ride – which really is not good for them, or for their creativity.

Just as creators demand perfectionism in themselves, they demand it in their managers. Inevitably this leads to conflicts, because creators' notions of the perfect rarely equate with managers' notions of the perfect. If the conflicts are repeated and incessant, they will not be able to work together: their styles are too mismatched. But managers never lose the respect of creators by complaining about their work being insufficiently original or creative. Managers only lose the creators' respect when they complain about their work being too different, or too radical, or saying that it does not follow established principles and guidelines. Then the creators know their very existence is being threatened, because they are being called upon not to create, but to repeat. All of which explains why the rejection of creative work is a matter which must be handled with care. (This will be covered in detail in Chapter 9.)

While leadership and challenges activate creators' perfectionism, to boost their motivation it is also necessary to massage their insecurities and egotism. (Robert Jacoby – then the exceedingly powerful, not to say autocratic, chairman of Ted Bates Inc., the second largest advertising agency in the world – once said to me: 'If people knew how much time I spend around here massaging people's egos they'd think I was crazy.')

Massage can be given in a variety of ways, though they all add up to much the same thing:

> Lots of cuddles. Very important. Verbal cuddles and physical cuddles. But certainly lots of verbal cuddles.
>
> (Paul Hamlyn)

> You have to flatter their egos. It is an enormous process of charming them, persuading them, treating them a bit like naughty schoolchildren. Of course I could mention creators who are not like that, but even in those there is still a little touch of the petulant ego.
>
> (Tim Bell)

> You have to have an attitude which is like a parent to an adolescent. You've got to be nice and you've got to keep on explaining. It's very trying on the nerves.
>
> (Wally Olins)

> They are childlike – not childish – in nature. And like children they endlessly seek approval.
>
> (Chris Jones)

> You endlessly have to cheer them up, to reassure and flatter them, and to establish a relationship of trust and encouragement, which is sometimes necessary to put them to work.
>
> (Jeremy Isaacs)

> If you approach musicians confrontationally they'll be confrontational. If you approach them respectfully they'll be respectful.
>
> (Alan McGee)

It must be added that good managers are not unsympathetic to the reasons for creators' need for flattery – as Jeremy Isaacs, for example, explains:

> It is all necessary because they give something that drains, they give more of themselves than other people in their daily working lives, and therefore are entitled to that little bit of extra support.

Similar views were expressed by Messrs. Grade, Jones, McGee and Puttnam – not to mention Gustave Flaubert – in the previous discussion of the creative personality.

To motivate creators, managers must also provide constant encouragement. Here are nine simple rules which can help managers win creators' support and enthusiasm:

- Absorb their risks – managers who encourage creativity must willingly and publicly take their share of the blame when things go wrong.
- Stretch organisational regulations – though managers cannot cavalierly disregard rules and policies, they must know when these need to be more honoured in the breach than in the observance.
- Be comfortable with half-developed ideas – it should not be necessary for every 't' to be crossed and every 'i' to be dotted before an idea is given consideration; and creators must have confidence that the manager can really understand and appreciate ideas at an early stage of gestation.
- Make quick decisions – managers who ho-hum and sit on the fence when shown creative ideas soon stop being shown creative ideas.
- Do not dwell on mistakes – mistakes are an inherent part of the creative process. Managers should ensure that creators learn from experience, but not make them wallow in it – 'I told you so' is an even more unappealing phrase to creators than it is to everyone else.
- Be a good listener – creators generally love to talk about their work, and managers have to love (or learn to love) to listen.
- Provide lots of feedback – creators are always eager for evaluation of their work, and since real results are often long delayed (and even then not necessarily precise) the manager must provide as much encouraging data, along the way, as possible.
- Accept trivial foibles – we have already seen that creators are not quite the same as everyone else; allowing them a few innocent quirks will stress your acceptance of their nonconformity.
- Defend them against attackers – in all creative businesses, creators are subject to frequent, and frequently unjustified, criticism; the manager must speak up, and be heard to speak up, loudly and boldly on their behalf.

If those are all positive ways to encourage creativity, here are 57 not quite lighthearted phrases which will block it, from Professor Michael Badawy's *How to Prevent Creativity Mismanagement*:

A good idea but ...

Against company policy.

Ahead of the times.

All right in theory.

Be practical.

Can you put it into practice?

Costs too much.

Don't start anything just yet.

Have you considered ...?

I know it won't work.

It can't work.

Too many projects already.

It doesn't fit human nature.

I've seen something like it before somewhere.

The client won't understand.

The timing is wrong.

There are better ways.

They won't go for it.

Too clever.

Too hard to administer.

Too hard to implement.

Too late.

Too much paperwork.

Too old-fashioned.

Too soon.

We have been doing it this way for a long time and it works.

It has been done before.

It needs more study.

It's not budgeted.

It's not good enough.

It's not part of your job.

Let me add to that ...

Let's discuss it.

Let's form a committee.

Let's make a survey first.

Let's not step on toes.

Let's put if off for a while.

Let's sit on it for a while.

Let's think it over for a while.

Not ready for it yet.
Of course it won't work.
Our plan is different.
Some other time.
Surely you know better.
That's not our problem.
The boss won't go for it.
We haven't the manpower.
We haven't the time.
We're too big.
We're too small.
We've never done it that way.
We've tried it before.
What bubble-head thought that up?
What will the customers think?
What you're really saying is ...
Who else has tried it?
Why hasn't someone suggested it before if it's a good idea?

There are, as can be seen, innumerable ways to stifle the uncertain germinations of a new thought. That is why it is so important to keep in mind Jeremy Isaacs' dictum that the role of the manager is to enable, not to destroy. There are times, many times, when ideas – bad ideas – need to be stifled. When it must be done it must be done clearly, positively and honestly, not with the kind of shilly-shallying weakness evident in most of the above euphemisms.

Motivation is a forward-looking process. The degree to which any individual is motivated to carry out a task depends upon the perception that carrying out the task will help him achieve the results he desires. So it might seem strange that in this discussion of motivation one all-important word has not yet been mentioned: money. There are two reasons. First, creators' attitude to their remuneration is not terribly different from other peoples'. Second, as has already been indicated, insofar as they are different at all, creators' attitudes tend to diminish the importance of remuneration as a motivating factor. That is not to say creators are not interested in money, far from it. They most certainly are. However, there appears to be no correlation whatsoever between the money they are paid and the resulting quality of their work. Unlike piece-workers, they cannot be incentivised to work harder by being paid more; their productivity cannot be geared to their wages. Yes, the best creators generally get the most money. But it happens that way round. The money is paid to them for their talent, not to motivate them to do better.

People who are really good aren't motivated by more money. They set themselves extraordinarily high standards. You won't get their standards to go any higher by saying 'here's some more money'.

(Chris Jones)

The best artists do not do it for the money. They do it for the buzz. They want to inflict their musical taste upon the nation, to hear their record going to number 1. And I want to inflict my musical taste upon the nation.

(Alan McGee)

Not quite everyone shares this idealistic, or at least passionately egotistic, view of creators' behaviour. *'It is generally thought,'* quipped the brilliant American advertising agency chief, Howard Gossage, *'that artists are interested in art. Nothing could be further from the truth. Artists are interested in money. It's the rest of us who are interested in art.'* But Gossage was being deliberately, if wittily, provocative.

'Ironically, the reward goldcollar workers want most – even more than money – is peer recognition,' claims Mark L Goldstein, and this is confirmed by other research which has been carried out to discover which factors are most significant in stimulating creativity among engineers and scientists (not, admittedly 'artistic' creators, among whom no such research has apparently been undertaken). In the survey the most important factors were, in descending order:

- Recognition and appreciation.
- Freedom to work in areas of greatest interest.
- Contact with stimulating colleagues.
- Encouragement to take risks.

The lowest-rated factors, also in descending order, are:

- Non-conformity tolerated.
- Opportunity to work alone rather than on a team.
- Monetary rewards.
- Criticism by supervisors or associates.
- Creativity training programmes.
- Regular performance appraisals.

Many of these points have been discussed above – though it is interesting to note how little value is put upon both training and appraisal. However, if the research has any validity, it seems clear that motivating creativity among scientists and engineers is different from doing so among arts creators in at least one central respect. Among arts creators the single most important factor is their perceived opportunity to fulfil themselves. This need for self-fulfilment derives from their egotism, their perfectionism, their insecurity and their craving for fame. It explains why, as we shall see in Chapter 9, they take criticism of their work so badly. To the manager it is the master key, with which all of their creative energies can be unlocked. Jeremy Isaacs explains:

> The most important way in which creative people are distinguished is by their single-mindedness, their belief that the beauty of a project, the excellence of a script or a film, has to be realised to the ultimate degree.

To return to Isaacs' definition of the creative manager as an 'enabler', if the manager enables them to do the work they want to do, to fulfil themselves, to create work of which they are proud and which others admire, the creators will work tirelessly in his service; and they will fight to do so. Here is David Puttnam's excellent analysis of the question:

> How do you motivate creative people? This is the crux of the issue. Give them confidence. Allow them to believe in themselves. Create an atmosphere where there is a sense that anything is possible, great work is possible. Part and parcel of that freedom is to be a master of technique. A large part of motivating creative people is to train them properly, so they have so much confidence in their technique – like a good driver behind the wheel – that they don't have to think about it, they need only think about moving on. A lot of people spend their lives obsessed by the inadequacies of their technique, and that is a tremendous stumbling block. I'm a great believer in training, and in the mentor ethos. You can be a brilliant darts player, and you can slog away in the pub day after day, but if you've not got anyone there nurturing you, correcting your errors, someone to criticise your play and encourage you, you'll hardly improve.

Lastly, on the subject of motivation, it is vital to remember that it is a constant, continuous process, not something that can be switched on with a counterfeit smile whenever the manager happens to remember. This is true of all management, but is especially true of the management of insecure and often prickly creators. So here are four precepts for managers to keep in mind whenever creators cross their path:

- Search for the praiseworthy – as Kenneth Blanchard and Spencer Johnson put it in their classic bestseller *The One Minute Manager*: '*Catch them doing something right*'. Search for the opportunities and they will be found.
- Praise the praiseworthy – maybe it is traditional British reticence (Americans don't seem to suffer from the same disability) but many

managers find it embarrassing to pay compliments when work is well done. When dealing with creators this is disastrous. Don't overdo it – if you gush too much and praise them too often or too easily, you will depreciate the value of the praise; nor, as you might hope, will it win you their affection. Occasional, enthusiastic and sincere praise is infinitely more valuable than incessant and over-enthusiastic slaps on the back.

- Reprimand rapidly – reprimands are as intrinsic to effective motivation as praise, provided they are accepted and understood by the creator concerned; this is why it is crucial not to delay them.
- Be specific – whether praising or blaming, concentrate on the particular work involved, and let the creator know as precisely as possible what is good/bad about it.

And as a footnote, never forget that one of the best motivators of all is to make creative work fun. Some psychologists have claimed that having a good sense of humour is an essential ingredient in the creative personality – but that is far from proven. What is beyond question is that many creators like to lark about when working together. ('*Most creative people are playful*' says Chris Jones). Playfulness relieves tensions, generates enthusiasm and relaxes the mind. Wise managers let it happen.

With so much motivation the creators should by now be raring to accelerate away. But unfortunately we are not quite ready to start moving yet.

SUMMARY

- The leadership of creative people must be earned; it will not come just because the manager has a grand title or status in the organisational hierarchy.
- The leader must ensure the creators understand, and share his vision – and he shares theirs.
- The leader must be, and be seen to be, a perfectionist who cannot be fobbed off with second-rate work.
- The leader must set tough challenges but also be liberal with ego-massage.
- The leader must provide constant encouragement, and various ways of doing so are listed.
- When the leader needs to reject work this must be done clearly and positively, not weakly with dissembling euphemisms.
- Money is important, as always, but it does not motivate creators to produce their best. Challenge and the potential for self-fulfilment are the motivators which drive them hardest.

- Producing great creative work should be fun, playful fun – and the good manager must not expect, worse still try to insist upon, the creators being deadly serious while they are working.

7

A Brief on Briefing

Is it only the idiosyncrasies of the creative personality that make the role of the creative manager so difficult? No. It is the nature of creativity. The manager wants the creators to produce something wonderful, something better than the competition, something that others will like and want and usually be willing to pay for. Yet at the outset neither the manager nor the creators have any clear idea whatsoever of what exactly it is they're going to end up with. As David Puttnam puts it:

> It is difficult to be precise with regard to the end product, because of the imprecision of describing it. When you start out you are describing something amorphous, which you are encouraging or asking them to create. That is a very specific management problem.

That initially amorphous something is the source of many of the dilemmas involved in the management of creativity. Because the manager does not quite know – cannot quite know, should not quite know – exactly what the creators will eventually come up with, the outcome manifestly cannot be precisely specified in advance.

In most walks of life managers give instructions to those whom they employ, whether they are employed within or outside the organisation. In Victorian times the instructions would be phrased as orders, and sometimes they still are. Today it is accepted management wisdom that employees work better if they are thoughtfully and sensibly instructed to do things, and if the reasons for the instructions are explained, rather than if they are given orders. Nonetheless the word 'order' still commonly applies in some quarters: in the army, in certain low-grade manual jobs, in restaurants (you give an order not an instruction to the waiter). Nowadays, however, orders generally apply to things not people. You order stock, or a car, or a widget. In most human situations instructions are the order of the day. But not in creativity. In the management of creativity the word 'brief', rather than either 'instruction' or 'order', is almost universally employed. Nobody instructs – let alone gives orders to – a designer, writer or composer. ('Instructions' may be given to the *corps de ballet* and the other foot-soldiers of creativity, but that is because they are not being asked to be creative.) People being asked to be creative are *briefed*.

It is useful to explore the differences between an instruction and a brief. Think about barristers, think about the law, where the word 'brief' has traditionally been used. The essence of a brief is twofold. First, though the eventual objective will be specified – 'I want to be found not guilty' – the way the objective is to be achieved is left almost entirely to the 'expert'. Second, although the client employs the barrister (through a lawyer) it is always evident that this is not an employer/employee relationship. Less still a boss/subordinate relationship. Using the term 'brief' ensures that the employer (the litigant) does not think he is in charge of the employee (the barrister).

Much the same applies in the management of creativity. First, the eventual objective must be specified, and we'll return to that, but the way the creator is to reach that objective cannot be specified. (If the objective and the way to achieve it are specified that isn't a brief, it's an instruction – or an order.) Second, although the relationship is that of an employer/employee, the word brief makes clear that both may have a similar status. One may be telling the other what is required but that does not necessarily make him 'boss'.

It is all but impossible to stress too strongly the importance of briefing in the management of creativity. If only it were possible for managers to give orders, or instructions, their lives would be so much simpler. But it isn't, though they frequently, and almost always foolishly, try.

The process of briefing in creative management is a great deal harder than briefing in the law. Objectives and results in legal situations are generally (though admittedly not always) straightforward and circumscribed. That is rarely the case in creative situations. Even formulating the brief in creative situations – let alone achieving it – is often immensely difficult.

Nothing causes more ill-will between creators and managers than the waste of time, effort, resources and imagination which are the direct and unavoidable consequences of inadequate briefing. Money is lost, tempers frayed, mutual respect dwindles to nil. Invariably each side blames the other. The managers insist that the creators failed (or didn't even bother to try) to understand the brief, while the creators insist that the brief was too vague, or incomprehensible, or downright wrong. Invariably the work has to be done again, and maybe again and again, in ever greater haste. The organisation incurs increased costs, other work gets delayed, clients and customers wonder whether to take their business elsewhere, and sometimes do so. There can be no doubt, to adapt the old military maxim, that time spent on briefing is seldom wasted.

Before even beginning to brief the creators the manager must establish the objectives of the operation. It may well be that part of the creators' task will be to help the manager define the objectives. So long as the manager makes it clear, this is a perfectly acceptable preliminary task. The manager will still need to do all the necessary homework beforehand. Remembering the manager's role as interface, he will need to find out what the clients or customers expect the creative work to achieve; what the organisation wants the creative work to achieve – in terms of sales or audience levels or whatever; whether there are no-go areas which must be avoided, or *sine qua non* areas which must be included. If it is impossible to stress too strongly the importance of briefing, it is almost equally impossible to stress too strongly the need for the manager to dig deep, to leave no stone unturned and find out everything he can about the project before the briefing begins.

Briefings can be written, or verbal, or both. (Some managers have strong views on this issue, to which we will return.) The objectives of all briefings are twofold. First, to let the creators know as precisely as possible what is required and to encourage them to excel. Second, to let them know, as precisely as possible, of any specifications or constraints within which they must work. To achieve the first objective the brief must inspire, enthuse and intrigue; the creators must be convinced that the project is in some way special, exciting and worthwhile. So the brief must be imaginative, stimulating and involving. Dull briefs produce dull work. To quote Chris Jones:

> Briefing should be directional – almost in a linear sense – and inspirational. It has to give as much impetus as possible

The second objective is similarly fraught because many specification details may be unknown at the start of a project, and may be intricately interdependent ('... if it's going to be printed in six colours it will need to be on this quality of paper, which in turn means using that kind of ink, which in turn ...'). At the point where all the details are known briefings transmute into instructions. That is, once the creativity has been achieved the process of detailed implementation may become a matter of simple – or not so simple – execution. (But it must never be forgotten that the execution of an idea is every bit as important as its conception.)

The exact nature and contents of a good brief will naturally vary from industry to industry. The brief for a new range of garments wil not be the same as the brief for a new television series. However all briefs should contain the following minimal data:

- Objectives: why is the project being undertaken? Who will benefit, and how? Is it intended to change people's behaviour? Whose, and in which ways?
- The target market: no creative project is ever directed at the entirety of the world's population. So is the target market national or international? Young or old? Rich or poor? In personality terms is it for conservatives or radicals, the fashionable or those uninterested in fashion, the emotional or the staid?
- Scale of project: is this to be a blockbuster in its field, or aimed at a small but specific market segment? Is it governmental, commercial or private? What are the corollaries in production terms?
- Competition: short and long-term – is this a competitive tender for a project, and if it is won what will be the real competitive environment in which it will eventually operate?
- Distribution channel: who is the initial customer/client? Will it need to win the support of retailers/distributors? What will be their criteria for acceptance?
- Style: is the project serious or light-hearted? Is it classy or classless? Should it be trendy or conventional? Should it seem expert or popular? Should it be explanatory or authoritarian?
- Communication: is there a message the public should take from the work? What is it? Will the message be controversial or conventional? Will it be political or apolitical? Might it be offensive? To everybody, to some, to whom?

The objectives, target markets and constraints will have now been defined with precision, leaving the creators with the right degree of freedom within which to flex their imaginations. At this stage the creators may wish to argue with the brief. Excellent. The good manager will encourage and may even provoke such arguments, because they help the creators to absorb and understand the brief more fully. If the creators raise valid arguments, it is crucial for the manager to amend the brief, despite the fact that this usually means getting the revised brief approved by others who had previously approved the original. Forcing creators to work to a brief which both they and the manager know to be wrong – a not infrequent occurrence, absurd though it may sound – guarantees garbage.

None of which should be taken to imply that creators abhor briefs, or the constraints within them. This is how Barbara Nokes, then Deputy Creative Director of the highly respected Bartle Bogle Hegarty advertising agency, put it:

The creative process is generally preceded by sheer terror. You're confronted with a blank sheet of paper and sharp pencil. You start with the brief, and the tighter the brief the easier it is to work to. If you know where the walls are you can travel down that narrow corridor and be completely wild. But if someone says it's an open brief you have no idea where to start.

Making a slightly different, but equally legitimate, point my ex-partner and creative director Paul Delaney, would say: 'If the client absolutely hates purple I want it in the brief. His dislike may be illogical, senseless, but I want to know. I may then rant and rave and say the client is an idiot, is crazy, that purple is the best colour, the right colour, the only colour for the ad. But at least I'll know the risk I'm taking right from the start. I'll know I'm in danger of wasting my time, everybody's time, if I insist on using purple. And I won't do that unless I am totally convinced there is no other option.'

Naturally briefs should always be as brief as possible. They should be sharply focussed and avoid all ambiguity. Creators, even more than the rest of us, get confused and discouraged if they have to wade through verbose and nebulous waffle. Managers who hope to give the creative imagination free rein by not mentioning constraints and limitations often believe, wrongly, that it is preferable for such constraints and limitations to be introduced into the project at a later stage, when it has more momentum. Very occasionally, this approach succeeds. Far more often it leads to imaginative ideas being mangled when they eventually collide with reality. The best creative managers do not hesitate to brief creators fully, warts and all, from the start. The limitations and constraints are part of the challenge, to which the best creators will respond with originality and vigour. Agreeing with Barbara Nokes, Tim Bell explains:

> The best way to brief them is to narrow down the area in which you want them to be creative. Give them as many facts as you possibly can, answer as many questions as you possibly can, so that in the end their area of uncertainty is so tiny they can allow their imaginations to explode within it. Lead them in one direction, give them nowhere else to go. You should never go to them and say, 'Have you got an idea about this product?' You must give them the selling idea, and then let them find a fantastically interesting and compelling way of expressing that idea.

And David Puttnam develops the point still further:

> The ultimate freedom for creative people is to allow them to work within specific and agreed bounds, bounds which they understand and appreciate. When I say understand, I mean they understand the reason for their existence. It's that thing about Pip in *Great Expectations* being told

to go and play. You can't tell a child to 'play'. You can give him two sticks and say, 'Would you like to go and play football with these?' and he'll say, 'I can't'. Or you can give him a patch of ground and a ball and see what he does with it. But you can't ask a child to 'play'. By the same token, I don't think you can just ask a creative person to create.

Note Puttnam's emphasis on agreement and understanding in the first two sentences. Some creative managers take an even more extreme view. Jeremy Isaacs sees good briefings as an open discussion at the end of which a consensus agreement about the general direction to be taken will have been reached:

If you want to explain to any group of people what some new project is likely to be, and to involve them, you have to explain it to them personally, you have to engage in a dialogue with them, you have to receive suggestions as to how the thing could develop, before deciding how you want it to develop, and then implement it.

Jeremy Isaacs is emphasising the involvement of the creators in the development of the brief. Wally Olins goes even further, arguing that briefing is not a once-for-all event but a continuous process of discussion and clarification which continues even while the work is progressing:

The way in which you brief creative people is not at one meeting. It is a delusion to believe that you actually give a brief to somebody. It doesn't happen like that. What you do, in my experience, is over a period of days, weeks and even months, work together with the person who is designing, the building or who is working on the identity programme, and you go through with them what it is that the client actually needs. The process of briefing is much more complex and more interactive than people believe. You get a great deal out of intense discussion over long periods about matters which don't appear to be germane, and only become germane when you see them in the context of the whole. Now that may be because the nature of my business is strategic and long-term.

And at this stage neither he nor Isaacs is keen on the use of paperwork, which they believe to be anathema to creators and stifle creativity. Olins says:

There's no point in writing memos, the creators won't read them anyway. And if they do read them they will resent it because they will see it as a directive and they will see themselves being maligned and persecuted by a vast bureaucracy which is designed to crush their creative instinct.

Isaacs makes much the same point:

Creative people can't possibly respond to a bit of paper that reaches them saying 'What we want to do is X or Z'. They can respond to a chat over a cup of coffee or a drink, in which you find out from them what it is they want to do ... I think all management that is done by paper is bad management. Management, if it involves dealing with human beings, which is what I take it to mean, rather than simply ordering things, is a question of human relations, a question of working with people. You cannot do that on paper.

Most managers, however, are anxious to commit things to paper, at the very least to confirm in writing what has been agreed, as David Puttnam explains:

Paper can be extremely useful if only to demonstrate to creative people the failure of their own logic. For example, if someone comes and sells me a project which is tremendously exciting but which has within it an area that worries me, I'll put that concern down on paper for them. It may be terribly valuable when you find out later that things haven't quite worked out. Creativity results from disciplined thinking. Paper helps you to create disciplined thinking in the artist.

Tim Bell concurs:

Briefs have to be written out, because otherwise everybody later disagrees about what was previously agreed. And memos are a bit more daunting than conversations. Perhaps my views are coloured because the copywriters I've worked with are impressed by the written word.

Even Wally Olins and Jeremy Isaacs, despite their fear that paperwork (which would naturally nowadays include e-mails) will suffocate creativity, accept that written instructions are needed at later stages in the creative process. Wally Olins makes the point clearly:

The short-term and immediate matters with which we are concerned derive from a whole programme which has already been created, and for these you have to have a tight brief. When you're producing something like a series of restaurants or a series of offices in a bank, and you have already done the strategic work, the technical work that you need to do falls into very tight parameters. And the briefing has got to be meticulous and accurately typed, and it has to deal with two things. In addition to the overall design strategy, it has to deal with time and money. No person in a creative business, as opposed to an artist, has any right to evade his responsibilities as far as time and money are concerned. If you evade your responsibilities for time and money you should not be in a business, you should be somewhere else.'

Time and money: the two thorns in the flesh of every creative manager. You may have spotted that they were, like the dogs that did not bark, inexplicably absent from the information to be included in any brief, listed above. That is because they need to be discussed at much greater length. Adhering to time schedules and keeping to budgets are key management functions in any industry, but in the creative industries – for perfectly logical and understandable reasons, which we will analyse in the next chapter – they are running sores, battles that must be perpetually fought yet can never be won. They are like evil gremlins inside every creative project, tinkering with the works, loosening the nuts and bolts so that at any moment it may career out of control.

SUMMARY

- Creative projects are unlike others because the outcome cannot be specified at the beginning.
- Creative people must be briefed, in much the same way that barristers must be briefed. The required result can be defined, but the route to reach it cannot. So detailed orders and instructions cannot be given.
- Briefs must inspire the creators to excel, while defining precisely the parameters and constraints within which they must operate.
- Creative people welcome tight and precise briefs, which make clear what they can and cannot do from the start.
- The manager must do all the research and homework necessary – usually a great deal – before even beginning to brief the creators.
- The manager should welcome, indeed provoke, debate and disagreement about the brief, because that will ensure the creators fully understand the brief and its implications.
- Whether or not the brief is initially committed to paper (or e-mail), initial discussions will quickly need to be followed up with written confirmatory details, and with precise factual specifications.

8

Time and Money

Although, as we shall see, there are disputes about this, in my view it is essential for time and money constraints to be incorporated into the brief from the very start. No matter how vague, how insubstantial, how visionary the initial discussions, it is vital for the manager to outline – if necessary in vague, visionary and insubstantial terms – the approximate financial scale of the project and an approximate time scale for its completion. As Barbara Nokes and several others have said, it helps the creators as much as the manager. It provides them, from the beginning, with a framework within which to exercise their flights of fancy. It provides them, from the beginning, with a reminder that the project is commercial, not pure art. It provides them, from the beginning, with realistic fetters with which to grapple, and to fight with if they deem it necessary. To repeat David Puttnam's maxim, *'The ultimate freedom for creative people is to allow them to work within specific and agreed bounds, bounds which they understand and appreciate.'*

Occasionally creative managers, anxious to provoke creators to levels of Utopian creativity way above and far beyond that ultimate freedom, say 'Take as long as you like, money is no object'. They never mean it. (If they do they should be fired.) They mean, but do not say: 'You are experienced creative people, so you have a pretty good idea of how much this kind of project would normally cost and how long it would normally take. On this occasion you can go over the top, because it is so important. And if you come up with the goods, somehow or other we'll find the time and the money. Within reason, of course. We've worked together before, so I know I can rely on you, and you know you can trust me. We all know what's wanted, don't we?'

To prove that is what is meant, it is only necessary to imagine the creators returning to the manager with a real 'time and money no object' proposal. How about: 'In order to carry out this project properly we'll need to work on it for at least 30 years and to do the work on planet Jupiter. Is that OK?' No, it will not be OK. 'Time and money no object' can be, to experienced creators, a reasonably clear if imprecise brief, which means, 'On this job you can exceed the norms by a fair margin in order to do something superlative'. Completely neglecting to mention time and money does not achieve the same result. (Nor should this be taken to imply that 'time and money no object' is an admirable brief – it is not. But used sparingly it can be an effective spur.)

As a project progresses detailed time and money specifications become, as Wally Olins said, absolutely unavoidable. And the more accurately they can be specified right at the start, the less likely it will be that important executional stages will need to be rushed, or carried out on a shoestring, towards the project's end, because too much time (often) and money (sometimes) have been frittered away earlier on.

Indeed as the project progresses the manager's attention to detail must be immaculate. No longer is the principal focus of his job the generation of soul-stirring creativity. The principal focus now must be accuracy and precision; getting the specification right in punctilious detail. As creative managers climb the ladder of success, they are able to concentrate, to an increasing degree on initial briefings, which are the most fun, and to delegate detailed specifications to subordinates. However, such delegation can only be accomplished safely and successfully if the senior managers have the key items in the specification in the backs of their minds. They will need to be aware of those items which could significantly affect timings and costs, and those items which could significantly affect the nature or quality of the end result. They will need the expertise to spot at a glance whether any of the specification details feels wrong, or could be symptoms of the evil gremlins at work. Few creative managers can get a feel for the rightness or wrongness of a specification unless they have produced such specifications themselves, when they were greenhorns.

This is an aspect of the creative manager's job that usually comes as a bit of a surprise to greenhorns. Less than amazingly perhaps, they expect the job to conform to its image: the thrills, spills and excitement of motivating creators. They do not expect to find themselves arduously completing detailed specifications, full of boxes and sections that demand to be filled in with sizes, weights and measurements of all kinds, with timings and costings and legal requirements and approvals. But they quickly learn that if such specification documents are completed incorrectly all hell will break loose, and it may break loose from several directions at once. The creators are furious because necessary information has not been supplied, or worse still has been supplied wrongly, so their work has been botched-up: the most heinous crime in their book. The senior managers are furious for the obvious reasons, but most of all because the creators are furious and senior managers spend their lives trying to keep creators calm and productive. The finance department is furious because money has been wasted and the customer or clients will be furious because their work has gone awry. And all because the specification wasn't filled in correctly.

Long before we get to the final specifications, however, the basic creative proposal must have been produced, and produced in the time allotted. As everyone knows, creative people are not necessarily good at timekeeping (and this may in part explain why others tend to view them as idle). *'Research shows that morning, noon and night are all the same to creative people; they don't work by the clock. Time has a personal, not a social meaning,'* states Professor Michael Badawy.

And psychologist Abraham Maslow observes:

> The creative person, in the inspirational phase of the creative furore, loses his past and his future and lives only in the moment, He is all there, totally immersed, fascinated and absorbed in the present, in the current situation, in the here-now, with the matter in hand ... This ability to become 'lost in the present' seems to be a *sine qua non* for creativeness of any kind.

Benjamin Franklin's well-known adage 'Time is money' might well have been coined for the creative industries – except that the creative industries hardly existed in Franklin's day. All industries own plant, hold stock, transform raw materials and suffer depreciation of capital, but in most of the creative industries the principal cost is human time. To quote another adage often heard in creative businesses: 'The assets go down in the lift and home every night'.

The assets naturally incur overhead costs, in addition to their own cost. The usual overheads of premises, travel, working materials and sometimes the specific overheads associated with their industries – film, fabric, instruments, technical equipment, computers and so on. Most of these overhead costs, though not all, vary in proportion to the creative time devoted to projects. More creative time means more overhead costs. Extra time means extra money. Every experienced financial controller in a creative organisation knows that when the creative time spent on a project is reduced overheads fall, as if by kindly magic; and if creative time is increased overheads grow, as if by black magic.

So controlling the time spent is a first and fundamental key to controlling creative costs. Time is of the essence. It is perhaps important to state at this point that some creative managers feel that controlling time costs among creators is not especially different from controlling them elsewhere. Consider what Paul Hamlyn, first, and then Michael Grade, have to say:

> Sure, timing is a problem, but it's also a problem with lawyers and accountants. You have certain people who do certain work for you, and you know they are very good, but they take their time. So you give them the sort

of jobs where it doesn't matter if things slip, by a month or two. If you have a deadline you don't work with people who can't stick to deadlines.

(Hamlyn)

I don't think keeping to time schedules is a function of being creative. Some creators are very good at it, some are appalling. Similarly, some are very good at administration, some can't cope with it. But that's true of all executives. I don't see any distinction about creative people. Likewise, some creative people are very good at controlling costs, some aren't, some treat it like their own money, some don't.

(Grade)

Michael Grade, however, adds an important rider:

Administration, money, budgets ... you can plug all these problems by giving the creative people support, so they can get on with being creative. You must never lose sight of the fact that what you are after is their creative flair.

The problem, then, is not that all creators are hopelessly and utterly incompetent about time and administration. Certainly there is nothing in the creative personality, as we have analysed it, which suggests creators are ordained by nature to be administratively inadequate. (Though it will be remembered that when they are working they tend to lose track of time.)

The problem is twofold. First, some creators who have exceptional talent happen to be administrative duffers. Second, the inherent nature of creativity – though not necessarily of creators – makes it uniquely difficult to tie results to time schedules.

With regard to the first, unquestionably there are many creative people who cannot get their adrenalin pumping, who cannot get themselves into top gear, until they reach the deadline. This is not unique to creators. It is a commonplace human trait. But it is especially prevalent, and extreme, among creators. As Christopher Bland puts it:

There are a lot of writers I know who admit that the truth is they never do anything until they're up against the deadline ... 'I don't start to get worried until it's Friday night and I'm going out to dinner and I know I've got to have it by nine o'clock the next morning. Authors are always late. Always, always late.'

David Puttnam and Wally Olins, recognising their own tendencies to procrastinate, are sympathetic to creators' difficulties. From his own description, Puttnam might well be one of Christopher Bland's errant authors:

> If I'm writing a piece for a newspaper I'll put it off and put it off and I'll persuade myself that I'm thinking about it, and that the longer I think the better it's going to be. The truth is you need the adrenalin to make you roll up your sleeves and sit down and do it. I often start at ten o'clock at night to do something for the following morning. I know it's wrong but ...
> (Puttnam)

> When writing books, I know that the deadline becomes an object I loathe and fear. In my mind, as I turn over the work, I decide it is impossible to meet the deadline, or if I do meet it I would be incapable of producing the best possible work. So within the creative mind you get this constant issue of the best being the enemy of the good. The creative man wants to make everything as good as he can, he doesn't mind if he sacrifices a month in order to improve things by three per cent. In other words, he loses his sense of proportion.
> (Olins)

Having thus identified the problem, Olins goes on to postulate the way the manager should tackle it:

> The job of the manager is: (a) to enable the creative man to lose his sense of proportion where necessary, and (b) to remind him that he has to regain it if he wants to earn money at the end of the month. That is a very difficult balancing act. There are plenty of hacks who will produce rubbish on time and within cost constraints, and what we have to do as managers of highly creative people is to enable the creative flame to exist in an atmosphere which is sympathetic. But they've got to understand that unless they operate within appropriate constraints of time and money, the company for whom they work will go broke. They have to understand that, and it's a very difficult thing for them to do.

We will return to the question of hacks in a moment, but this general approach to time management is widely accepted. Tim Bell says:

> I have a very simple view about it. We're not in art, we're in business, and there are deadlines. One of the reasons why creative people are paid large amounts of money is because they are supposed to understand commercial disciplines. That means 'Have an idea by Thursday'. It may seem impractical, it may seem unfair, it may seem that you're likely not to get the best results – and all of those things may well be true – but the fact is that we are working in the world of commerce, and in the world of commerce there are deadlines that have to be met.

David Puttnam agrees:

> Obviously in the making of a feature film timing is critical. Time really is money. So we are very precise in terms of the number of days, hours, minutes and seconds things are going to take. If they start to go too high, things are adjusted quickly – preferably before the actual filming starts.

That brings us to the first absolute rule about the control of time and all other costs on creative projects. It was implicit in Puttnam's earlier advice that creators should always work within *specific and agreed bounds, which they understand and appreciate*. The rule is: don't impose time schedules, agree them in advance. The word 'negotiate' is almost more apposite than the word 'agree', since there are frequently tussles between creators and managers about the length of time any project will take. The creators – seeking perfection – want more time; the managers – knowing time means money – want them to have less. However, as so often in the management of creativity, there are likely to be complex cross-currents in evidence: the creators will want to finalise the work as quickly as possible, and win the expected acclaim, while the managers will want them to have as long as is reasonable to produce their best work. A good management rule of thumb is to get the creators to state their ideal requirement, and then to lop off 20 per cent (one day in five). This will stretch the creators without causing undue strain; and if the ten day job truly cannot be completed in eight days – a rare occurrence – the creators can be relied upon to say so. Vehemently.

That, however, is an extra twist. The essential principle is the advance agreement, as Christopher Bland and David Puttnam point out:

> If the creative people are involved at the beginning, then there have to be exceptional circumstances for things to over-run. For the creative people it simply means going through the no doubt very tedious process of agreeing everything in advance, working things out, making sure they really think they can do it and then sticking to what's been agreed.
>
> (Bland)

> The system I use is consistent discipline, and supplying an optimum amount of information from the outset. I give the creative people all the information they can possibly want, so they can never say, 'I didn't know that'. They are partners, and since it is a genuine partnership you have got to share aims, and share problems.
>
> (Puttnam)

Why then, despite everyone's best efforts, do creative projects so often over-run? Why are creators so particularly prone to procrastinate?

'The time necessary for rehearsals,' aphorized Bertolt Brecht, *'is always one week longer than the time available.'* Naturally creators share mankind's love of indolence. But as we have seen, their personalities push them towards being workaholic rather than idle. They tend to delay because being perfectionists, as Wally Olins said, the best is often the enemy of the good. They reject their own good ideas in an almost manic determination to do still better. It is not at all unknown for creators to throw away marvellous work which they don't feel to be good enough, which others then rescue from their waste paper baskets or from the cutting room floor, late at night. That is not something which occurs in accountancy or personnel management.

The difficulty is accentuated because, as David Puttnam said earlier, you are 'asking them to create something amorphous' – something which does not yet exist. The same is not true of, say, bottle manufacture or transport management. Production lines run at predictable speeds, journeys take a fairly predictable time. Nothing much changes from week to week, or month to month, so the managers can identify exactly how long things will take; and when things do change, the consequences of the change are usually calculable. Creativity isn't like that. Every project is a new project. Experienced players can estimate roughly how long things will take, and tough managers will ensure they take no longer; but that does not mean that the timing of creative work can be equated with the timing of bottle production. (That is why hacks, to pick up Olins' earlier point, find no difficulty in delivering on time: they produce their work to rote, without being creative).

At first sight it might seem strange, as Tim Bell put it, to demand of anyone that they should have a great, original conception for a new fabric design, or a television programme, or an advertisement, by next Thursday. But that is the nature of the industries in which creators work. Successful creators must be able to originate good ideas to order; and the more fecund the creator the faster he will be able to do so. Many of the world's greatest artists have produced masterpieces at an astonishing rate of knots. Mozart and Shakespeare were hardly slouches, and Balzac and Dickens churned out their serialised novels to unforgiving monthly deadlines. So it can be done, even at the highest levels of creativity.

The manager who constantly suspects that creators who are not overtly creating must be idling is more likely to stimulate paranoia than outstanding original work. The great novelist, William Thackeray, for example, described himself *'sitting for hours before my paper, not doing my book but incapable of doing anything else'*. Managers should never underestimate the neurotic niggling that nags ever more obsessively in the creative mind as the deadline approaches and the great creative solution has not yet been conjured up.

The question at the heart of most creative time problems is: what is the value of perfection? *'There is hardly anything in the world,'* claimed the great critic and social reformer, John Ruskin *'that some man can't make a little worse and sell a little cheaper.'* Or do a little quicker. And in the creative industries the converse is also true: there is hardly anything in the world that someone can't create a little better, but it may cost a great deal more. As Ruskin implied, defining the price, and value, of quality is a universal problem and always has been. In most industries, however, it is possible to calculate with considerable accuracy the cost-effects of quality improvements, or impairments; and to make at least an approximate estimate of the likely effect upon consumer demand. Modern market research techniques can now help companies make such estimates with a fair degree of precision. Computer analyses can help companies investigate the probable results of a wide variety of adjustments to costs, margins and prices, no matter how complex the inter-relationships between the various factors involved. With the exception of personnel decisions, few if any major business decisions are made today which do not involve the study of computerised predictions of the possible consequences. A very large number of business decisions can be reduced to mathematical analysis, and though the computer cannot make the decisions, it is an invaluable guide – particularly in the area of cost control.

Almost none of this applies to creativity. No computer can, or ever will, be programmed to tell you whether one design will be better liked than another, whether one orchestration will be more popular than another, whether one actress will be better in the part than another. No computer can, or ever will, be programmed to tell you whether two subtle colours harmonise or clash, whether one adjective will be more telling than another, whether one type of brick matches another or does not. At certain stages in most creative projects, market research can be employed – if the scale of the project justifies it, which many don't – and may provide rough guidelines, as we shall see. And of course computers are used throughout the creative industries, to handle and process all sorts of routine data. But the infinite majority of tiny decisions that have to be made on every project – size of typeface, shade of blue, timbre of sound, use of punctuation, and so on are, must be, and forever will be, taken subjectively and quickly. This is another crucial point about arts creativity which differentiates it from other industrial activities.

From the manager's point of view, he must rely continually on the creator's judgment. It is the creator's role to make all the minuscule decisions which in total constitute the entire project. Success will depend on their ability to make such decisions correctly. The great majority of the decisions – size of typeface, shade of blue, timbre of sound, use of punctuation – have no cost implications. But others do, and if the cost implications are of significance, the manager must know, and must be involved in the decision.

As with time schedules, the absolute rule about all costs is that they need to be agreed in advance. And as with time schedules, there are often complex cross-currents at work, as Jeremy Isaacs here points out:

> You have to have gone through the budget with several tooth combs from the word go, and to have satisfied yourself that the project can be made within budget. That often means increasing the budget so that at least you know you have made a realistic commitment ... 'We are kidding ourselves if we think we can get it done for that, it will end up twice over budget. So if we want to do it we are going to have to resign ourselves, from the word go, to the fact that that is what it is going to cost.'

Creative people sometimes resist that – they say, 'No, no, it won't cost anything like that, I wouldn't dream of asking you for that much'. They are nervous that if it is going to cost 'that much' the manager is going to say, 'No, we can't afford to do it'. And they are right to be nervous. It sometimes happens. But from the manager's viewpoint it is essential to get the budget right, and it has to be built on realistic assumptions.

> I think that the fatal, dreadful and irresponsible thing for the creator to do is, either by secrecy, or by tunnel vision or by megalomania, to drive a coach and horses through financial barriers. That is a disgraceful thing to do and should never be tolerated by any organisation.
>
> (Isaacs)

Christopher Bland wholeheartedly agrees about the importance of involving creators early in budget planning:

> Television cost-consciousness has grown very considerably in the last few years. Programme budgets used to be regarded as guesses, not things to be adhered to or to be taken too seriously. Now programme budgets are looked at very hard and they are looked at by the creative people too. Budgets used to be something the accountants did, and the creative people thought: 'We'll make the programme and they'll tell us whether we overspent or underspent'. It would rarely be the latter. Now there is more creative involvement in the active planning of budgets.

However, the initial problem, as Isaacs implies (and returning to John Ruskin), is how to set the original budget, given that the best will cost more, and no computer will be able to give you even an inkling of whether or not it will be worth it. Like the spotting and selection of talent, these decisions will always be judgmental, be made on the basis of instinct, hunch and experience. That does not mean that they should be either random or illogical. The crucial issue the manager must perpetually keep in mind is the total amount in the budget, whether the items under consideration can be met within it and, most important of all, whether the eventual income – be it sales revenue, fees or whatever – will fully cover that cost.

This is how David Puttnam perceives the problem, expanding on the above discussion of the importance of detailing the target market in the brief:

> The game I play as a manager is: can we tell the story in such a way as it will interest and reach a large audience – in which case it justifies large resources. Or are we going to attempt something which maybe has its own integrity, but which is likely to reach only a small audience and so justifies only a small budget. A most interesting case in point was *The Killing Fields*. Despite its subject matter, we decided to aim the film at the optimum potential audience. We acknowledged and took on board certain compromises. And we made the film accordingly. It was a successful decision. We made the same assessment on *The Mission*. But we didn't carry it through. We never really solved the problems of the film in its first 25 minutes and the film never recovered from that. You've got to be honest with yourself when you are asking for resources. You've got to be able to say to yourself 'with a fair wind and with a decent bit of luck, I will be able to recover, recoup and repay those resources.' That's the job of the manager, and sometimes you go wrong.

Jeremy Isaacs' approach is not too dissimilar, though from a somewhat different perspective:

> First of all, you have to operate within your own total budget. You have to operate within your own resources. If you don't operate within your own resources as a manager of a creative institution you will bankrupt the institution and put yourself out of a job. You then roughly apportion those resources between the different projects that you know you have in the schedule in a particular year – one or two of them you may allow, within the available budget, to approach as near perfection as possible. You decide to back this one all the way. That is a purely subjective judgment: I'm going to back these people all the way. Other people I'm going to ask to work within sterner financial constraints.

If you back people all the way and they deliver something that is both creatively unsuccessful and also commercially unsuccessful, you've made a very bad judgment indeed, and if that is your track record you're not going to be a very successful manager. If you make such a judgment and the thing is creatively successful and commercially unsuccessful, well at least you've got something you can point to with pride. If you're hugely fortunate and come up with something that is both creatively successful and commercially successful then you get medals. But those are very difficult managerial decisions, and I have to say that luck must play a certain part. The important thing is never to allow the down side, the risk of any potential decision going wrong, to be so all pervasive as to destroy what you are trying to do.

All of these analyses reflect the manager's Janus-like role. He is aiming to balance the creators' ambitions with the requirements, and the potential, of the marketplace. The manager's overall strategy – the desired outcome – will define the total resources that can be afforded, the total costs that can be justified. It is within the total that the tiny decisions will be judgmental, as David Puttnam relates:

> You have to make judgments. You have to assess whether you are dealing with something that's truly important, or just something that's ego-based and whimsical. Visconti on his sets would put very, very expensive china in the cupboards even if nobody ever opened the cupboards. He believed it enhanced the way the actors performed on set. He once purchased 12 silk shirts to go into a drawer, which would never be seen – so that Burt Lancaster, playing his role, would feel his hand slide between the silk shirts when he went to the drawer to pull out a purse.

Patently, Visconti's financiers had decided, in Isaac's phrase, 'to back him all the way'. Equally, knowing Visconti's style, they doubtless built the cost of his little extravagances into the original budget, if they were doing their job correctly. Chris Jones relates a similar tale of perfectionism driven to uneconomic extremes:

> I worked with an art director in the 1980s who designed a completely new typeface for a small campaign, and had it made. That was before the days of computer typesetting, and producing the face cost about £35,000. Over £100,000 today. The client refused to pay of course. So it was a write-off. It would be hard, even impossible, to prove the public had any idea a special typeface had been designed. If I'd known about it beforehand I'd have stopped it. And I'd have been right. I admire his perfectionism. But it went far too far.

Jones's story highlights a basic problem. Once the costs have been agreed, how does the manager ensure that the creators do not, like Michael Cimino, like his art director and like a million others throughout the creative world, drive a coach and horses through the barriers? This is an issue in which the cost-per-project is inextricably bound up. And so, not infrequently, are lawyers.

Low-cost projects rarely merit intricate cost and time controls. The cost of the controls might easily exceed the cost of the project. The manager must trust the creator to operate within the constraints agreed, and establish through experience – as Paul Hamlyn explained – which creators require latitude and which do not. The smallness of the job in no way abrogates the necessity for prior agreement about timing and costs – almost the reverse, since once the items have been agreed the manager may well pay no further attention to them until the project is completed. If he then meets unpleasant surprises he must make his displeasure known, forcibly. The nature of low-cost creative projects inherently means, as has been pointed out, that there will be lots of them. The manager must adapt his style accordingly. Precedent and consistency are all-important. So are continuing relationships, as manager and creators move from job to job, each learning the other's weaknesses and strengths. It is perhaps because Paul Hamlyn and Michael Grade have learned to do all this instinctively that they feel, as they said at the beginning of this chapter, that controlling creators is not that different from controlling other people.

High-cost projects must be handled quite differently. All the managers involved in high-cost projects agree it to be essential to appoint financial supervisors – whatever their title – to keep a close and watchful eye on the creators' progress. Here are three clear statements of principle:

> You can't expect creators to administrate their own expenditure. You've got to give them really competent people to monitor what they're spending. Preferably production people, because then the creators feel they're sympathetic, rather than accountancy people who they think are the enemy.
>
> (Tim Bell)

> You need systems of financial control whereby certain expenditures can only be authorised by the positive act of a responsible manager, and where all expenditures against budget are reported to a central financial control system at the very least weekly and ideally daily. Then when things begin to go wrong – like we've only got a quarter of the footage shot for this

movie and we've spent half the budget – you get some advance warning and you can move in to try and get control.

(Jeremy Isaacs)

To control costs you must put a really tough accountant on the production, who won't let them overspend, and who will control things all the time. Because if he doesn't you'll get an over-run. Even if he does you may get an over-run because he can't control every aspect of the process. He will monitor costs on a daily basis, but what he can't monitor is the value of what's in the can, relative to producing the whole thing. He will know X amount of footage has been shot, and Y is the budget, and he's got Z left to play with. What he can't know, is when the director will say: 'I can't use that ...' after it's already been shot. He just can't monitor that. Nobody can. If you're making a series you should know within the first week if you're over-spending. If it takes two or three programmes, two or three episodes to discover, then you're in real trouble, somebody's cocked it up. It isn't necessary. You ought to be able to discover weekly. It's not difficult. You may choose to ignore it, that's your prerogative. But if it takes two or three programmes then you've got very bad control systems.

(Christopher Bland)

This is something Jeremy Isaacs confirms from his personal experience – an example, to reiterate his earlier point, of the advantages of having worked on both sides of the fence:

I always tried to work within budgets and quite often in my life have had to work within very severe time constraints. I mean you just have to finish by a certain date because the programme is going out every week. I found that the single most difficult thing to do. When I knew I had something that wasn't good enough, and that a really creative fellow wouldn't have done, I nevertheless knew it had to be broadcast on Wednesday. Halfway through *World at War* it turned out it was going to cost in the end twice what I'd estimated it would cost.

But I wouldn't have fired myself for that. Because of the reporting of costs system, I was able to take my employers along with me. And it was already apparent, when two of the programmes were finished out of 23, that other companies were beginning to be interested in buying them, and that Thames Television was going to make a great deal of money out of the series. Therefore, they could perfectly rationally decide: it now looks as if it's going to cost 2X rather than X, but we can see that what we're getting is something that we very much want.

Isaacs was perhaps lucky because *World at War* was, deservedly, a phenomenal success. That is by no means always the case when budgets are overspent. The making of *Heaven's Gate* is a supreme example of creators disregarding agreed schedules. The director over-ran at every single stage: after 12 days shooting the picture was ten days behind. The film finally opened about two years late. This is Steven Bach's description of how such calamities occur:

> It is not unusual – it may even be routine – for a picture to experience difficulties in the early days of shooting, particularly when the work is on location. If the picture is a big one and the conditions are in any way primitive, these problems can grow geometrically or exponentially ... Every picture is different from every other picture and has its own unknowns, its own problems, requiring solutions often unique, often without precedent for those who are expected to deliver considerable ingenuity on critically short notice ... Accordingly, if experience in the movie business teaches anything, it is that it doesn't teach everything.

As was mentioned previously, United Artists, who were backing *Heaven's Gate*, felt themselves in a weak position *vis-à-vis* the director, Michael Cimino, because they desperately wanted his then glittering creative reputation to bolster their tarnished one. But as Puttnam has stressed, when creators gain the whip hand over management, disaster will surely ensue. *Heaven's Gate* became a *cause célèbre* precisely because everything about it went so outrageously wrong. Fortunately, few creative projects go off the rails so wildly. In part at least, that is because managers have developed the scheduling techniques necessary to control them. Wally Olins summarises cost control problems thus:

> It's up to the management of the organisation to manage the business properly. When you get to a phase where you're doing a job and the creative people say, 'We're worried we're going to go over budget because we need to produce something but we haven't got enough money', and the client says we can't have any more money, I may well say we will take a loss on the job because we have to do it right because that's the ethos of this company. The good manager of creative people has to judge when to go on and on, and if necessary go way over budget. And if you get it back you get it back, and if you don't you don't. Sometimes it's worth it, and sometimes it is simply a bloody waste of time, self-indulgent rubbish.

The point Olins makes about *'the good manager of creative people has to judge when to go on and on, and if necessary way over budget'* – as Isaacs did on *World at War* – is the essence of the problem. It is relatively easy to state, as many of my contributors have done, and as textbooks invariably do, that once budgets have been agreed they must never be exceeded. But it isn't *quite* true. In the music business recordings frequently go disastrously over budget, when musicians re-record and re-record repeatedly and incessantly. But sometimes the end result is worth it. Alan McGee states:

> I allow people to be perfectionist. We take a more liberal view than other record companies. We let the artist be the artist. Then they feel they've got to deliver. I'll put people under pressure, but I'm very very pro artists. And they know that.

It's a high risk strategy. But it is one that has resulted in many great – and financially successful – works of creativity, in all fields. If overspending budgets always ended in disaster things would be easy. But it doesn't, so things aren't. In the management of creativity it is possible to give guidelines, but in the end the manager's judgment is everything.

And extra costs can creep in even after a project is nominally finished. Note, for example, this memo about the film *Funny Girl*, written by Alan Hirschfield, then President of Columbia Pictures:

> Now that this picture is completed the most difficult job all of us have is holding down additional expense. It appears to me that the cost could rise substantially if the producer is allowed to have free rein of continuing expenditure. At some point someone is going to have to say no to some of the requests or all of the very good efforts that were made to hold down costs during production will be overshadowed by the post-production expenditures. I believe it is very important that a very hard line be taken in this regard.

Why are creative budgets so frequently overspent? The problem reflects another key to the heart of the management of creativity. Because the end product is 'amorphous' before it is started, the possibility must always exist that it could be improved while in progress. Improved commercially that is, not just aesthetically to please the creators. If the manager keeps a tight clamp on the costs he risks diminishing the commercial potential of the work. Despite this, the basic rule must stand: costs must be clamped. On the other hand, as everyone knows, rules are made to be broken – very, very, occasionally.

There is, however, one area of cost control where the rules must never be broken: the control of rip-offs. There is no data to prove the point, and there probably never could be, but it seems that rip-offs – particularly bribery and expense-account fiddles – are more prevalent in certain of the creative industries than in other commercial fields. In the record business corruption was rampant in the past, but appears to be less common now. In the movie business cheating is still widespread. According to knowledgeable people in the film industry bribes, payoffs, and other financial improprieties run into millions of dollars annually. All of which is often euphemistically called 'creative accounting', but it is not an aspect of creativity with which the wise manager will want to have much truck.

Finally, a visiting Martian might ask, why can't all these intractable difficulties be resolved by lawyers, with well drawn contracts that will ensure things are completed on time, without rip-offs and within budget, and that ferocious penalties will be exactable if they are not? That, after all, is how things are done in other industries. Well as has already been stated, the creative industries do spawn more than their fair share of contracts, and *in extremis* contracts sometimes help. They can stop things going totally and completely awry. But, day to day, they are rarely a complete answer.

First, the 'amorphous' problem again raises its nebulous head – courts find it hard to decide whether or not creativity has been completed to specification. Second, contracts are much more effective as a means of stopping people doing things than as a means of forcing them to do things, particularly when it comes to forcing them to be creative. Third, the costs per project are frequently far too small to warrant the involvement of expensive litigation. Fourth, legal processes are so slow that it can be months, and often years, before judgment is given – and still more costs are then incurred. Fifth, exacting financial penalties from individuals is hideously difficult – if the creators don't pay, would they be imprisoned? Sixth, which creators would want to work for organisations that might incarcerate them?

Even the best designed control systems in the end come down to personal relationships and personal involvement, as Jeremy Isaacs explains:

> You just have to keep saying 'We've only got three more weeks left, Bill, we've only got two more weeks left, we've only got one more week left, three more days left, and we can't go on for a week longer because the money for that extra week isn't there'. It's endless chivying to get finished on time.

Happily the problems are not quite so overwhelming as any chapter which concentrates upon them must inevitably make them sound. For as Wally Olins neatly puts it:

> There is a spectrum. There are a number of highly creative, highly imaginative people who are self-disciplined, who manage themselves extremely well – and are therefore extremely easy to manage.

SUMMARY

- Time and money are the two most important constraints in the management of creativity, and the most difficult to handle.
- The time and money available for any job must always be indicated on the brief from the start – even if they cannot always be defined precisely at that stage.
- As things progress the time and money specifications can and must be refined, and committed to paper in detail.
- It is vital for the manager to get the creators to debate and accept the time and money constraints in advance, not to impose them. Without such acceptance financial disaster is almost inevitable, but even with acceptance the manager will have to work hard to ensure they are not exceeded.
- Timings run into difficulty because creators lose their sense of time when engaged in creative thought – and because, like everyone else, they procrastinate. But the manager would be wrong to think that just because they cannot be seen to be 'working' they are not working.
- For low-cost projects the manager has little choice but to rely on the creator's self-imposed controls.
- For high-cost projects it is essential for financial managers to be integrated into the day-by-day operational structure, preferably financial managers who the creators will find congenial, but more vitally managers who can stay close to what is going on at all times.
- Despite such tight controls overspends will occur, and managers must use their judgment about what then to do. Sometime overspends eventually pay-off.
- But that must not be allowed to negate the basic rule that budgets are fundamentally sacrosanct. (Flexibility is an essential factor in creative management!)
- The manager must always be on the look out for rip-offs, which are commonplace in the creative industries.
- While legal contracts are essential they can only be brought into play *in extremis*. Generally they can be little more than a backstop; a protection against things getting completely out of hand.

9

Yes, No, or Maybe

At last. The creators have finally settled down to work: sketching, scribbling, typing, gazing unseeingly into the distance, struggling to nudge their personal muse into life with every wile and ruse at their disposal. They now know what is required, who the target is, how long they've got, how much they can spend, and all the constraints within which they must work. Should they be left alone? Or should the manager drop in on them now and again to see how things are going?

There is no universal answer. It depends on the creator, not on the manager. The standard textbook advice is that the manager should not try to get involved too soon. Professor Peter F Drucker, one of America's foremost management gurus, supports this view unequivocally:

> The best thing you can do for creative people is just get out of their way.
> Give them a task and leave them alone.

Unquestionably there are talented creators who resent, and cannot cope with, having to explain ideas which are still in gestation. Sometimes this is plain cussedness, but sometimes it is an unavoidable consequence of the way they work. Typists and bricklayers generally start jobs at the beginning and work through to the end, but many creators proceed haphazardly as new thoughts occur to them. There are excellent scriptwriters who habitually work back from a punchline, and nonetheless succeed in creating a convincing story. PG Wodehouse wrote his chapters in higgledy-piggledy order and blended them together as the book took shape; John Cleese has described how he and Connie Booth wrote each of the *Fawlty Towers* episodes, constructing the plots on huge sheets of paper and reorganising them again and again; prize-winning novelist John Irving starts by figuring out the end of the book, then works backwards, beginning each chapter from the rear as well; we have already seen how Mozart would build a whole symphony in his head, before committing it to paper. None of them, it may be assumed, would have responded warmly to zealous managers asking them to 'show me how things are getting on'. They could be expected to endorse, as would many creators, Professor Drucker's advice.

Not all creators seek such solitude, however. Some need constant reassurance, and like to show people their work frequently during its development. Naturally they prefer to show their work to those whose opinions they respect. Nor do they always accept the opinions they receive. Lots of excellent creators continually 'test the water'. They invite criticism, listen, consider it thoughtfully, and then reject 99 per cent of it. This may be frustrating for the critic, but can be hugely beneficial to the creator. It helps him to see his work through others' eyes, and to probe its strengths and weaknesses.

The varying ways in which creators work may reflect basic differences in their personalities, as Dr Anthony Storr spotlights:

> Artists who are predominantly of depressive temperament may, like Michelangelo, produce masterpieces over which they have had to labour for years. The less gifted, or the more deprived, may not be able to tolerate long intervals between obtaining the supplies of self-esteem which they need. Some writers, for example, are so driven to produce short works in rapid succession that they never do themselves justice. The immediate rewards of journalism are seductive in this respect. Seeing oneself in print every week, or even every day, is immensely reassuring to some characters. But this need for recognition carries the disadvantage that it may preclude the production of more serious, lengthy work. Many journalists cannot face the long period without reward demanded by writing a novel. They 'want it now'; and having found a way of getting it cannot give up this source of immediate satisfaction.

Creators working within a large organisation can, to some degree at least, get the best of both worlds – if their psychology so demands. They can take the time necessary (or anyway the time permitted) to do the job to the best of their ability, and seek regular 'supplies of self-esteem' along the way. Supplying regular doses of self-esteem, like insulin to a diabetic, is part of the manager's job. And most managers welcome it because it allows them to keep an eye on the work as it progresses, and to reassure themselves that it is on the right lines.

Creators who prefer to labour alone, like hermits, and emerge from their seclusion with the creative work neatly parcelled-up and finalised, give managers sleepless nights and nervous breakdowns. However, as Dr Storr implies, the differing working methods of different creators are embedded deep in their psychology. So managers who try to force the hermits to keep presenting their work before they are ready – or conversely, managers who refuse to look at work which is incomplete, even if the creator asks them to – will soon find those particular individuals unwilling and unable to work with them. Creators do not come in uniform psychological shapes and sizes. The manager must be sufficiently flexible (and flexible does not mean weak) to adapt his style in order to help them optimise their output.

If he has sufficient power and authority, however, the manager can take a conscious and explicit decision not to work with particular types of creators, or with creators who work in ways he finds unacceptable. Inevitably, this will preclude him from working with certain individuals, some of them perhaps highly talented, who are unable to work in the way required. Wally Olins has made exactly this kind of decision. The way his company operates demands that creators work openly and that the fruits of their labour are available to continual inspection. It will be remembered from Chapter 6 that his building has been designed specifically to facilitate such openness. (*'We don't want a situation emerging where people are secretly working for days or weeks, nights or weekends ...'*) This is one of the company's basic precepts:

> That is the way the company has always worked, from the very beginning. Anyone who comes into this company is not told those are the rules, they see those are the rules. And whatever they learnt before they have to forget. Because peer group pressures here are so great. There are teams of people, and these teams keep on inspecting one another.

Without question, Olins' system offers considerable advantages, particularly with regard to the amendment and rejection of work, which we will be considering further in a moment. However, there are also disadvantages, as he himself admits:

> The teams keep changing. Everybody is working in the open. If somebody's a bastard then everybody knows he's a bastard, and everybody says he's a bastard, and they say, 'Do I have to work with that bastard?' ... Sometimes it isn't worth paying a high emotional price for talent, and you have to get rid of them.

Were Olins willing, or able, to allow the talented 'bastard' to hide away somewhere, in a cubbyhole, he might conjure up ideas which, in William Wordsworth's inspired line, 'flash upon that inward eye which is the bliss of solitude'. He might contribute immense creativity to Olins' organisation, without antagonising and alienating members of a team. However, the employment of such loners would not be compatible with Olins' approach to briefing, and perhaps even more importantly, would raise other management problems which Olins' system successfully solves. Creators' personalities haven't changed. Titian and Rubens were

111

great team players – and team leaders – while Caravaggio, arguably at least as fine an artist, would fulsomely qualify as one of Olins' bastards. It is worth adding, in support of Olins' views, that Titian, Rubens and their studios were, in consequence, infinitely more prolific than Caravaggio could ever have been.

It is often said that creators 'take criticism badly'. That is generally true, though few human beings I have ever met take criticism that well. It is one of humanity's many little inadequacies. With creators, however, the inability to take criticism is especially apparent, because they are continuously 'being judged by their output'; and as we have seen, they view their output as an extension of themselves, as a reflection of their character and their ego. When the manager criticises one of their creations, he is not criticising some abstract artefact. He is criticising them. This is clearly recognised by most creative managers. Jeremy Isaacs, for example, explains it thus:

> It's only natural they should take rejection harder because they put so much of themselves into what they are doing. They do not put their work forward in a routine sort of way, they put it forward in a very serious kind of way. So you have to be very, very certain that when you propose a change to somebody you have very, very good reasons for it.

Christopher Bland's views are similar:

> You have to do it and recognise that it is painful. It's a highly subjective and therefore rather bruising process. It always boils down to 'I don't think it's good,' or 'I don't think it's good enough,' or 'I don't think it's any good at all'. However you dress it up, however good your creative credentials, it is very painful for the guy on the receiving end. That's true whether it's a piece of copy, or a manuscript for a novel or a piece of film, whether it's documentary or drama. You have to tell them. Telling them why is hard. You can't say, as you can with the iron foundry casting, look it's the wrong size, or it's got holes in it. With creative work it's a subjective judgment. You have to say, 'That doesn't work,' or 'It doesn't look right,' or 'It doesn't hold together'. Try telling an actress that her voice isn't right, that she's not performing well. It's very bruising.

Nonetheless it must be done. The importance of rejecting unsatisfactory work has already been stressed. From the creator's point of view the manager must act as leader, controller, critic, and demander of excellence. What has not been stressed is the importance of quality control from the customers' point of view. As the interface between the creators and other people – usually the customers – he will have to answer to them if the creative work is unsatisfactory. And often the manager will need to persuade them that the work is right – sell it to them, either personally or indirectly.

But however good a salesman the manager is, and however glib his tongue, he should never attempt to sell creative work knowing it to be wrong and knowing it could be improved. Sometimes things aren't that clear. Sometimes the manager will have an uneasy feeling about the work, a feeling that it isn't quite right, that maybe it could be better – but will be unable quite to pinpoint why or how. On such occasions he must rely on the creator's judgment, and must present their work to colleagues and customers with as much confidence as can be mustered. Such uncertainties are inherent in the nature of creativity. As Christopher Bland has emphasised, it is a subjective business. There are probably no creative products about which absolutely everyone agrees. All of us see films, watch television programmes, hear records and gaze at fashions about which we are unable to make up our minds. The manager, however, is not paid to be indecisive. So if he cannot make up his own mind he must rely on the creator.

In any case, such indecisiveness should be rare. If the manager is capable of doing the job, he must be able to decide, quickly, whether the creative work meets the brief. Notice the phrase 'meets the brief', since this is a frequent source of contention between creators and managers. In an ideal world – or so creators would have it – managers would take responsibility only for the 'content' of creative work (the brief), while the creators themselves would be responsible for its 'form', or style. 'Aesthetic' decisions, the creators argue, are outside of the competence of the manager, and so must be the prerogative of those with the necessary talent to make sensitive judgments – other, more senior, writers and designers perhaps, but not managers.

To some degree, most managers accept this point of view. On the other hand, the manager knows that customers and colleagues will not be too bothered about the metaphysical dividing lines between content and form. If those concerned do not like, and won't accept, the humour of the TV series, or the designs of the fabric, or the style of the magazine, they will not be mollified by being told that the brief was carried out correctly in all other respects. Hence, the manager is forced to become involved in the aesthetics of creative projects. The extent to which he feels the need to do so will depend, in great measure, upon the trust and confidence the manager places in the creators working on the project. This boundary between form and content in creative work, between creative and managerial responsibility, is, and forever will be, a verbal battleground.

As long as both sides are evenly matched and respect each other's competence, the outcome will be superior creative work.

Here Michael Grade, supporting Christopher Bland's viewpoint, describes encounters which all managers of creativity will immediately recognise:

> It's difficult to argue logically about whether or not colours are right, and it's just as difficult to argue about characters on a page. It's all subjective. It's all, in the end, about choices and tastes. Every kind of creative decision is about choices and tastes. So those subjective arguments occur with all kinds of creative people.

If the manager is asking the creator to alter a piece of work, rather than to start again, it means the manager has found a kernel in the work which he suspects could be turned into something much better: he is saying 'maybe'. The good creative manager will deliberately foster his own ability to spot gems buried in debris. More important still, he will be able to redirect the creator's enthusiasm, so the gem will be polished to achieve its maximum effect – not thrown away, often by its creator, in a welter of temperamental dissension.

Professor William G Kirkwood, of East Tennessee State University, in a passage entitled, 'Learn to Build On Ideas As Well As Criticise Them', describes this process:

> Remember to actively look for the strengths in any idea you or others develop. As weaknesses become apparent, don't dismiss a concept altogether; seek ways to correct its flaws while retaining its strong points. This can be done using a three-step process.
>
> When you wish to respond to an idea, first note its strengths. True, the idea might not be right in its present form, but are any parts of the concept useful? Are the goals of the idea positive, even if more work is needed to achieve them? Does the philosophy that inspired the idea seem to be on the right track? Only after you've identified the concept's strengths should you address its shortcomings. Last, for each weakness you see, develop a means to overcome the flaw while preserving positive features.

That final piece of advice is one about which many experienced creative managers would have misgivings. All would agree that it is desirable to look for strengths and positive features before looking for weaknesses and shortcomings. But, in Britain at least, most creative managers prefer to hand the job back to the creators for amendment, rather than try to improve it themselves, or even jointly with the creators.

As Jeremy Isaacs says:

> If you're inclined to do it yourself, you're in desperate trouble.

In my own experience, 'improvements' which are agreed in meetings, during often over-heated discussions, rarely prove to be improvements when reconsidered a few hours later. I therefore strongly resist the pressure to find solutions in groups. That, however, does not contradict the essential requirement to provide criticisms which are as detailed as possible. Tim Bell explains:

> As far as amendment is concerned, my technique is to confront it with detailed comments: 'Isn't there a better piece of music?', or 'Couldn't we cast somebody better?' or 'The dialogue's not very tight,' or 'That third line doesn't add an awful lot'.

That is the manager espousing his correct role: re-setting the problem, the challenge – not demotivating the creators by offering (probably uncreative) solutions of his own.

If the work cannot be usefully amended, is beyond salvation, the manager must bite the bullet and throw it out. Rejection involves three common difficulties. First, too much time has already been invested for it to be possible to start again. Second, too much money has already been invested and the waste would be unaffordable. Third, too much of the creator's ego has already been invested, and to start again would be hideously painful. None of those constitutes an acceptable excuse for going ahead with a dud project; yet dud creative projects frequently go ahead, after they should have been stopped, for one, or another, or all three reasons.

With regard to the first two, it is the manager's responsibility to allow for contingencies within the original plan, which was drawn up at the briefing stage. Managers all too frequently rely on creators hitting the nail precisely on the head first time. It is reasonable to expect carpenters to strike nails home accurately, every time. It is unreasonable to expect creators to produce brilliant ideas likewise. Creators who fail repeatedly end up in dire straights. Until that point a degree of cautious indulgence is necessary, and delays must be built into the schedule, but not be publicised. (Nor should the manager lie about it. Lies get discovered. The manager must simply state when the job is needed – and that's that.)

The same is true of financial reserves. The manager should provide for them, but not publicise the fact – as contingency funds have an unhappy propensity to evaporate once their existence is known. No manager can, or ever should, attempt to insure against every possible type of disastrous delay and bungle; but all managers should keep a little in hand and be ready to expect the unexpected. On major projects consideration should always be given to taking out professional insurance cover, if the premiums are not excessive.

With regard to the third difficulty, it may be unpleasant, but the manager cannot afford to be fainthearted. David Puttnam states:

> Creative work must be rejected quickly and cleanly. It's not something to dwell over.

Michael Grade and Christopher Bland agree:

> There's only one way to handle rejection and that's to be absolutely blunt and honest and clean. You can't let people down lightly. You have to say, 'Look I'm sorry, we're not going to do it for this reason or that reason'. Rejection's got to be handled on the basis of straightforwardness and honesty.
>
> (Grade)

> You just have to do it, and recognise that it is painful.
>
> (Bland)

Tim Bell, while not denying the necessity of handling rejections firmly, finds a tiny bit of dissembling helpful:

> You are not allowed to say, 'I don't like it,' as the basis for your rejection. That is one of the fundamental disciplines for anybody managing creativity. You can say whether you like something or not, though even that you have to be careful of, but you must certainly not make the fact that you don't like it the reason why it shouldn't go forward. Your rejection has to be on rational, logical and strategic grounds rather than emotional grounds.

Paul Hamlyn and David Puttnam agree with Bell, that it is desirable to make the rejection sound objective rather than purely subjective. Michael Grade and Christopher Bland emphatically disagree. Here are Grade's views:

> I would never do that. I would give reasons. I would say, 'I think it's too expensive for what the return is,' or 'The risks are too great,' or 'You

haven't got this right,' or 'This is no good'. Then you have a dialogue. But at least you're arguing from the basis of honesty.

Whichever way you handle it, and different managers obviously approach the problem in different ways, rejection must never be baulked. Only idiotic managers, with no sense of priorities and no interest in their own long-term employment, will allow poor work to be progressed because they are unable to overcome the difficulties involved in killing it.

Wally Olins has deliberately structured his systems to dissolve away many of the problems of amendment and rejection.

If you operate in a structure such as ours, where you have constant meetings, where you regularly see what is going on and you are absolutely honest with each other, then you won't get to a situation in which there is an internal presentation at which creative work is rejected ... The physical layout of this building is such that people have to talk to each other all the time, and show people their work.

Olins even makes the same system succeed in his relationships with clients:

Nothing will go forward that the client would not like because we go through the development process internally and we go through it externally, too. The client is constantly involved in the development of the idea. The manager's job is to persuade the client that the idea is right, and it may be necessary to spend months doing that.

Olins' approach is initially very time-consuming and therefore, expensive. However, among the greatest costs of all creative businesses are the costs of rejection. The costs of beginning again; doing the same thing twice, three times or more; bringing new creators onto a project where others have failed; along with the problem of sapped morale and dwindling confidence – all these factors added together, Olins believes, will far outweigh the cost of doing things correctly (if expensively) in the first place.

It is obvious that not all creativity could be handled under Wally Olins' system. It is rarely, if ever, possible for photographers and journalists, or authors and composers, to be constantly supervised or to work in teams. Nor, as we have seen, is the system acceptable to all creators; nor would the cost-per-project always justify such a level of management involvement. But his principles could be more widely applied, and with considerable success.

Probably the most important single thing to keep in mind through all the rational and emotional difficulties involved in criticising creators' work is that the likelihood is that you are – and want to be – locked into a long-term relationship. If you have decided the creator is not up to par, or not your style, then naturally your behaviour matters less. (Though there is never any excuse for being downright nasty.) But the great majority of manager/creator relationships are continuous, over lengthy periods, and no creator will pull out the stops for a manager he has discovered lies to him constantly, or is unpleasantly brutal, or does not listen to arguments. Creators quickly learn which are the managers they can trust.

For that reason, among others, the manager should always aim to minimise the pain inflicted by handling the situation as subtly and sensitively as possible. This is not always easy. Tempers often run high. It is not unknown for verbal fisticuffs to explode into real fisticuffs (Though in my lengthy career I have only seen that happen once – and even on that occasion the punch-up could, and should, easily have been avoided.) To minimise the frictions, here are five rules which will help make the unpalatable marginally more palatable:

- Be at pains to be fair – point out the good elements in the work, as well as the bad; and make clear that you are sympathetic to the problems.
- Control your non-verbal communication – non-verbal communications often say more than the words we use, especially to perceptive creators; this is particularly true during criticisms and confrontations, when they are looking for tiny glimmers of reassurance and support. Remember Paul Hamlyn's cuddles.
- Do not rush – the creators have probably spent a long time on their work, and it is of much importance to them; do not reject it after a second's glance, or indeed without a second glance.
- Seek areas of agreement – try hard to get the creators to understand and agree to at least some of your criticisms, otherwise they are likely to harbour resentments which will later blossom like tropical plants in a hothouse.
- Summarise conclusions – because such meetings can be emotional, it is crucial to clarify at the end just what has been agreed, and what is going to be done, without bullying, but to resolve any muddle; and it is usually a good idea to confirm the conclusions in writing soon afterwards.

When the unhappy meeting is over, Blanchard and Johnson offer the following advice in *The One Minute Manager*: '*Stand up, walk with the person to the door, and make a fleeting but encouraging physical contact*

– putting your arm quickly around the person's shoulders is best.' It may sound irksome, and by British standards a bit gooey, but it works wonders with creators who have just been battered about a bit.

SUMMARY

- Some creators prefer to be left alone while they are creating, others seek constant appraisal and encouragement.
- Neither approach is right, or wrong; the manager must adapt his style to the personality of the creator – though managers naturally tend to prefer working with creators who keep them in touch with jobs as they are progressing.
- Because creators view their output as part of themselves, they take criticism particularly badly; and this is exacerbated by the subjective and personal nature of most criticism.
- When criticising, the manager should first search for good points buried within the work, which it may be possible to develop or refashion to make the work successful.
- It is almost always preferable to ask creators to refashion their work out of, and after, the discussion rather than attempt to make improvements 'in committee'.
- Even if the work could never be amended sufficiently to make it acceptable, the manager should praise aspects that can be praised, before rejecting it in its entirety.
- There will often be strong, pragmatic arguments in favour of accepting dud work, but they must be resisted.
- Consideration should be given to devising an organisational system in which creative work is constantly scrutinised and appraised by (a) the creator's peers and colleagues, and (b) the final client.
- It is essential for managers at all times to keep in mind that most of their relationships with creators are not one-offs, but will be relatively long-term.
- This makes it essential to win the creator's trust and respect – and not to act in ways that would inevitably lose it.

10

Researching Creativity

With characteristic perversity the marketing of creativity is almost the exact antithesis of the marketing of all other goods and services. Indeed, purists might argue that the marketing of creativity is not really marketing at all.

The accepted textbook definition of marketing describes it as a process which begins with the consumer and tracks back to the manufacturer. First, consumers are asked what products they want; the manufacturer then develops products he believes will meet those wants; the manufacturer then tests the products on the consumers; only then, if and when the products are acceptable, does the manufacturer produce them and aim to persuade consumers to buy them. This seemingly logical process rarely proceeds in quite so orderly a fashion in the real world, even outside of the creative industries: but it is the paradigm to which marketing executives today aspire.

In the creative industries things mostly, and inevitably, happen the other way around. Having received a brief the 'manufacturer' (that is, the creator) decides what to produce, and then, via the manager, aims to persuade consumers to buy. In this sense, the creative industries are production-led rather than marketing-led, and they always will be.

Unquestionably the best and most successful creative organisations pay close and continuous attention to what their customers want. They use their experience, intuition, flair, hunches and judgment. They use their eyes, ears and – though rarely in the olfactory sense – their noses. They study trends and fashions with far greater concentration than their peers in other industries. They have no choice, because for them change is perpetual, change is of the essence. However, they do not ask consumers what they want; nor – with one or two exceptions, which we shall note – do they test their products on consumers prior to production. In other words, they do little or no product research. To marketing people in other fields this would be anathema: the antithesis of true marketing.

The reasons why managers in the creative industries normally eschew 'product' research are twofold – one: cost-effectiveness, and two: effectiveness.

The cost-effectiveness reason derives directly from the earlier cost-per-project analysis. The vast majority of creative projects are far too small to bear the cost and/or the time, necessary for market research. Fashion garments, one-off television and radio programmes or mini-series, music, records and books could very rarely justify the investment on a product-by-product basis. In effect, the way publishers, broadcasters, garment manufacturers and the rest do their market research is by generating a large number of alternatives, quite inexpensively, and seeing which of them the public take to.

But the second reason the creative industries do little market research is more fundamental. Research is a notoriously inaccurate means of assessing consumers' future tastes in creativity.

First, in many instances creative industries seek to lead and change tastes rather than follow them. It is impossible to pre-test next year's fashions, or next year's musical sound. The fashions or the sound, will only take off if they are promoted with a great deal of press and television publicity (equals hype); if they are accepted and adopted by opinion leaders and if their mood and tone match the mood and tone of the moment. None of these crucial factors can be built in to prior product research. If, to take a simple example, a glitzy film star finds a particular garment fetching its sales are likely to boom forthwith. Unfortunately film stars rarely reveal their future apparel – rarely know their future apparel – and so cannot show it to market researchers so they can then show it to the public and garner their responses.

Second, the great majority of individual creative products are bought by tiny minorities of the population. There are very, very few books, records or fashion garments which sell in millions. One million people equates to just over 2% of all UK adults. Market research techniques are not nearly exact enough to identify with any precision the tastes and requirements of so small a minority. If the results were inaccurate by 1% – ie the research registered the 2% as 1% or 3% – the inaccuracy would represent half-a-million people.

Third, for a majority of creative products there is a chasm between concept and execution (as was explored in Chapter 4). The precise ways in which any idea or concept is executed will greatly effect its acceptability. So that while most other consumer products can be tested out in concept form, in advance of production, most creative products cannot. Consequently creative products must usually be 'manufactured' before they can be tested – by which time many costs will already have been incurred, and many decisions irrevocably taken.

Fourth, for many, if not most, creative products the most powerful sales generators are critics and word-of-mouth publicity. This is unarguably true in the movie, book, music and fashion industries. The companies involved seek as much publicity as they can, and sometimes bolster it with paid-for advertising. But these efforts merely kick-start the fly-wheel. Without the support of critics and/or word-of-mouth publicity, the flywheel soon grinds to a halt. There is no market research technique which can simulate critical acclaim or word-of-mouth publicity; and even if there were, there is no way of knowing in advance whether or not any particular creative product will successfully garner them. The way in which word-of-mouth publicity sold *The Full Monty*, and failed to sell Kevin Costner's massively expensive *Waterworld* are stories that have often been told. (In the record industry, TV and radio plugs are the equivalent of word-of-mouth publicity – the mouths, in this case, belonging to the disc jockeys.)

Fifth, whereas consumers in most product fields can describe with reasonable precision what they want a product to do, and criticise with reasonable clarity the failings of products they do not like, the problems of specification and analysis in creative fields make this all but impossible. We have already seen that even experienced managers of creativity find it difficult to specify creative projects in advance. (It's the 'amorphous' problem once more.) In most creative industries, those who can respond to the products and describe their reactions become the critics mentioned in the previous paragraph: the fashion, music, cinema and architectural correspondents of newspapers and magazines. Or they become style gurus. Ordinary members of the public, often lacking the necessary vocabulary, can say what they like and dislike, but cannot be expected to analyse their opinions in depth. To quote Richard Birtchnell, then at the Burton Group:

> Ask the consumer directly to nominate designs, styles and colours and few will be able to tell you. The best you can hope for is, 'I need something for a dinner party'.

To overcome, or rather outflank, all these difficulties, several creative industries have become extremely proficient at rapidly gauging consumer response to new products in the stores. The leading garment and record companies, for example, obtain immediate day-by-day computerised sales data, usually from a carefully chosen panel of retail outlets. Future sales can then be predicted with a fair degree of accuracy. Manufacturing orders can be instantly geared-up or geared-down, to be ready either to meet heavy demand or to minimise over-production. To quote Birtchnell again:

> To operate successfully in the fashion business you need to be clairvoyants on surfboards. What the surfer does is go out into the ocean feeling for the

waves, and when a good one comes along he paddles like hell to get onto it. Then rides it for all its worth before it goes crashing into the rocks.

Nonetheless, and despite the formidable problems, some of the creative industries do engage in product pre-testing, when the cost-per-project makes it worthwhile, or even imperative. The three industries which most use such market research are movies, advertising and more recently television. The techniques are not universally or unequivocally accepted; they have not eliminated the risk of failure, far from it; there are many case histories of occasions when tests have clearly miscarried; there are also many case histories of projects on which they have clearly been of assistance – *The Full Monty* again being a celebrated example.

In the film industry, new movies are occasionally pre-tested at concept stage when the script has been drafted and putative stars chosen, but before a final commitment to filming has been made. Such testing was more commonplace in the 1960s and 1970s than it is today. It has fallen out of fashion partly because of some notorious occasions when it has gone spectacularly wrong. The concept of *Star Wars* is said to have done poorly in pre-research, and as a result the film was rejected by two major film companies. Likewise, *ET* tested badly and as a result was turned down by Columbia, before being accepted by Universal and becoming the most successful motion picture of its time. In both cases, the gap between concept and execution was one with which the research techniques could not cope. If the films had not been made as well as they were, they might indeed have failed. The fact that they were made well emphasises the vital influence that the quality of a creative product's execution has on its chances of success. And thus emphasises the fallibility of such concept tests.

Almost every major movie, however, is nowadays screened after it has been filmed, but before it is launched publicly. This is because the costs of promoting and distributing movies are now so huge – about one-third of the total cost of a Hollywood feature – that it may be better to ditch a film, and carry the loss, than to compound the loss by launching the film in the marketplace. (Every year hundreds of completed feature films fail to get big screen distribution, and get shown only on television or video). In both the United States and Britain the research companies which specialise in movie research have, over the years, amassed sufficient data to enable them to compare the test performance of each new movie with hundreds of predecessors. The sample audience is interrogated with questionnaires that have been honed, over time, to provide clear and useable responses. As well as *The Full Monty*, which was almost completely remade as a result of such research, the ending of *Fatal*

Attraction was reshot three months after filming had been completed. Most film production contracts now include a contingency allowance for the extra filming that will be necessary if the research so indicates.

Equally importantly, these test screenings identify which sectors of the population enjoy the film and which do not, and why they enjoy it or do not. Publicity, advertising and promotional material can then be aimed precisely at the appropriate target market, with the appropriate message. Managers in the movie industry now have considerable faith in the power of test screenings to gauge both the size and the nature of the target market and to reveal why the film appeals to them. Major television series, particularly in the United States, are now subject to very similar processes.

No creative industry, however, is subject to as much research as advertising. Again this is a consequence of the high costs-per-project involved – though it must be understood that from the advertiser's point of view the cost-per-project is the total cost of the entire campaign: both the cost of producing the advertisements and the cost of the space or television time. Moreover, the commercial importance of getting the advertising right is increased beyond its own cost, because of the effects it can have on many other aspects of the advertiser's business: sales, manufacture, economies of scale and the rest. (The knock-on influence of packaging and other design work is similarly important, which is why designs and packaging are also increasingly being tested.)

Innumerable weighty tomes have been written on the topic of advertising testing, and more and more appear each year. It must therefore suffice here to say that, as with films and television, advertisements can be tested both at initial concept stage and after they have been produced. The advantages and disadvantages are much the same in each sector. However, advertisements, unlike films, have no purpose in their own right, but are created in order to sell products. So the key factors which advertisement pre-tests aim to gauge are whether they are memorable and whether they are persuasive. It is comparatively easy, though quite expensive, to measure the former. It is impossible to measure the latter, so various surrogate assessments have been devised which deal with the question obliquely, but do not provide an exact answer. The data suggests that the measure which provides the closest relationship with sales effectiveness is likeability. Eight separate academic studies have shown a relationship between likeability and effectiveness. However, it should be noted that 'likeabilty' is not a synonym for 'amusing' or 'entertaining'. Consumers like advertisements for a host of reasons – including being informative – and similarly dislike them for a host of reasons, including being irrelevantly funny.

In addition to films, television and advertising, other creative industries which carry out a certain amount of market research into their products are packaging and design, as has already been mentioned, plus newspaper and magazine publishing. Many magazines have carried out research into the impact and sales effectiveness of their covers, and more recently book publishers have started to test jacket designs. (Magazine covers and book jackets are both forms of packaging.) Newspapers, and especially magazines, often produce and test 'dummies' of potential titles, in the style, shape and size of the proposed publication. The *Independent* was extensively researched in this way before its original launch. Designs are printed in very small quantities, or handmade, for test purposes.

In all creative testing, whatever the product or service, the closer the prototype is to the final product, the more reliable the results. Whenever the project is tried out in rough, conceptual form, the research findings must be interpreted with great caution.

Finally, on the subject of pre-testing creative work, it is worth noting the research methodology used by *Reader's Digest* publications, as it has often achieved exceptionally high levels of predictive accuracy. By normal publishing standards, *Reader's Digest* books are blockbusters: the costs-per-project (and the anticipated sales) can run into millions. So the Digest can afford to commit considerable financial resources to its pre-tests – which are done in stages, from initial name and concept through to the finally bound, printed and priced volume. At every stage the book is revised, and sharpened, in the light of the findings. Over the years, as in the film industry, the Digest has built-up a sizeable library of data, so that new projects can be compared, as they progress, with those that have gone before. And from the comparisons predictions can be made.

The validity of the 's research system is not due merely the meticulous care with which it is carried out, important though that is. The difference between the Digest and other publishers is that the Digest both sells its books by mail and carries out its research by mail. In other words, the research technique exactly replicates the sales method used, in terms both of creative content and target market. For the tests, the Digest draws upon a representative sample of those households which it eventually intends to mail and then sends them descriptive leaflets which approximate more and more closely to the sales literature which will finally be used. Any creative business which sells its products by post could employ the same techniques, and some mail-order clothes companies already do so, albeit on a lesser scale. But the great majority of creative organisations, which sell their wares in less controllable ways, are unable to take advantage of such tightly controllable tests.

In any event, even the Digest willingly admits that the finest research techniques available are no substitute for editorial flair. The research can provide aims and directions, but the creators must produce the goods. Similarly, the movie marketing people acknowledge that test screenings can uncover the faults in a film, but only the writer and director can correct them.

Most creators' attitudes to market research are equivocal. On the one hand, they value, indeed are often thrilled by, the general public's opinions of their creativity. They enjoy the very notion of people looking at, concentrating upon and discussing their work. On the other hand, they firmly believe that the general public has neither the perspicacity nor the sensitivity to criticise their work meaningfully. They subconsciously feel the public should respond to their work emotionally, without being required to analyse and dissect it. This is how Tim Bell, perhaps exaggerating a tad to make his point, describes advertising creators:

> They're completely blind to the consumer. That's something they have in common with newspaper editors and television men. All of them have this arrogance, that it is not necessary for them to know what the people they communicate with think. Or rather, they think they know already, without checking. They just don't feel it's necessary to check. When you do some research into an idea, or a piece of advertising, and the findings show people didn't understand it, the creators reply. 'They should have done'. They're like football players, who want to be seen to be playing football better than each other, and they're less interested in the opinions of the crowd, or the opinions of the manager, than in the opinions of each other.

In the advertising industry, where testing is held to be of great importance, a new breed of specialists has come into existence whose principal function is to act as an interface between market research and the creators. These specialists, called account planners, are researchers who are particularly sympathetic to creativity. Their job is to test creative work among the general public (or the specific target market), and then to report the research findings to the creators. Good account planners – and it is surprisingly difficult to find individuals able to fulfil the role – help the creators to understand and accept research findings, even findings which are highly critical. (There is no problem in getting creators to understand and accept research findings which are laudatory). Some researchers in the movie industry have a similar role, though it has not been identified as a specific and separate job function. In those other creative industries where the testing of creativity occasionally takes place, it is the manager's role to smooth the communications path between the creators and the research.

At last the creative product is right, or at least as right as the manager and the creators know how to make it. It is time for it to be sold. At this point each of the creative industries goes its own way. Films are not sold in the same way as fashions, books are not sold in the same way as television programmes, buildings are not sold in the same way as greetings cards. Indeed, even within each industry different companies and organisations go about their marketing in completely disparate ways. Creativity is essentially a production function: creators are employed to produce things, not to sell them.

Nonetheless, certain consistent strands do appear to run through the promotion and marketing of many of the creative industries:

- Advertising is often of little importance – advertising-to-sales ratios are minuscule in the books, records, fashion, design, television programme and even movie industries; and the creative industry which uses advertising to promote its goods least of all ... is advertising.
- Sales are greatly influenced by journalists and critics, whose comments in both public and specialist media are highly influential – the manager should ensure that he knows as much as possible about the significant commentators in his field, and wherever possible get to know them personally.
- Publicity in the creative industries is frequently generated by the staging of events to which the journalists and critics feel impelled to come – premieres, parties, fashion shows, stunts. People within each industry get bored and fed-up with such events but they must never be neglected; on the contrary, as much effort as possible should go into making them bigger, better and more original than competitors'.
- Word-of-mouth publicity, as has already been stressed, is always of massive importance – and this can be stimulated, to some considerable degree, by the originality and impact of events and stunts.
- Opinion leaders, as has likewise been stressed, are also exceedingly influential in most creative fields – this is partly because the public is uncertain of its creative tastes, partly because the activities of opinion leaders keep them, and the products they use, in the public eye. For the manager, the employment of opinion leaders offers considerable publicity potential; very few are impervious to sponsorship.
- Diversity is an essential element in the marketplace – as we have seen, it is inherent in the nature of creativity, that people seek variety. Singularly few creative products gain even one per cent market share, insofar as it is possible to define market shares. The manager must therefore always be working to offer his market as

much variety as it needs, rather than aiming to dominate it with one or two products. To quote Richard Birtchnell once more: 'The individual's aspiration is to appear unique, but as fashion retailers we are only profitable if we sell in bulk'. The paradox is common throughout the creative industries, and is an essential component of any marketing strategy.

The above six points are characteristic of the creative industries, and to a great extent differentiate them from other consumer goods industries. Other consumer goods industries normally depend on advertising; critics and journalists hardly ever write about them (with the exception of cars and financial services); critics and journalists rarely attend product launches; opinion leaders are quite unimportant – who knows which detergents or toothpaste they use? – and in the majority of markets a few brands hold a dominant market share between them, which is what most marketing people aim for.

To round off the subject of marketing, managers should always keep it in mind that creators look to them to sell their work, and feel bitter if they fail. Paul Hamlyn puts it anecdotally:

> You are telephoned in the middle of the night and asked: 'Why isn't my book on sale at Paddington Station?'

There are exceptions – as there have been in almost every aspect of creativity management – but by and large creators do not like selling their own work. They do not think themselves to be much good at it, and they are not. So the manager who they know can sell their work wins their trust. Tim Bell says:

> The real reason creative people have respect for you is that you've got the guts to go and sell their work. And you can sell it better than they would be able to.

Marketing executives are prone to boast that how a business goes about its marketing will define the structure of the business. Without doubt the ways in which creativity is marketed mould the structure of the manager's role. In industries where the requirements of the customer can be discovered and defined with some precision, the manager can transmit those requirements in clear instructions to the producers of the goods. Nobody would dream of arguing that the customer's requirements should not be met. In the creative industries the customer's exact requirements can rarely be predicted, and can never be defined with any precision. So the manager is always second-guessing. He is second-guessing the customers when briefing the creators, and second-guessing them again when the creators present their work for acceptance. The manager permanently walks a tightrope, with the uncertain demands of the marketplace on one side, the uncertain output of creators on the other. If either side becomes too turbulent he will be blown off balance. To be a successful creative manager it is essential to be as adept at coping with customers and colleagues as at coping with creators. It is essential, in other words, to be a dab hand at marketing creativity as well as at getting it manufactured.

SUMMARY

- Although all creativity must be produced for its marketplace, the creative industries are production-led rather than marketing-led.
- Compared with most other modern consumer industries, the creative industries engage in comparatively little market research; they rely to a very great extent on experience, intuition, flair, hunch and judgment.
- Market research is difficult throughout the creative sector because creativity creates new trends and fashions whose acceptability is difficult – sometimes impossible – to test out in advance.
- Market research is hardly used in low cost-per-project sectors like books, fashion and music because it would not be cost-effective; it is cheaper to launch projects and see if they take off.
- Market research is used more extensively in high cost-per-project sectors like movies, television series and advertising.
- Pre-testing is particularly difficult because the way a project is executed and publicised will hugely influence its popularity and success, and those factors cannot be simulated.
- Post-testing is more accurate, particularly when research companies build up databanks, so that the results achieved by each new project can be compared with those achieved in the past.
- Most creative people accept that they are not salespeople, and rely on managers to do the selling for them.
- The marketing of creative products is different from the marketing of most consumer products in at least half-a-dozen ways.

11

Fun and Profit

'*If you're not in business for fun or profit, what the hell are you doing here?*' quipped Robert Townsend in his iconoclastic management classic *Up The Organisation*. We'll return in a moment to whether or not the management of creativity is fun; indubitably it can be profitable. The top managers in advertising, newspaper and magazine publishing, television, sales promotion, movies, records and fashion all earn more than a handsome crust. Marjorie Scardino's £1,000,000 or so pay cheque from Viscount Cowdray's Pearson Group is exceptional, but not that exceptional. Book publishing might be thought to be the Cinderella of the creative industries; but fortunes can be made even in book publishing, to which the publishers on the list below bear witness.

Twenty three of those named among the top 200 richest people in Britain in 1999 listed in the *Sunday Times* – marginally more than 10% – work as managers in the creative industries, and that excludes Sir Paul McCartney joint 33rd in the chart with £500 million), Sir Elton John (138th with £160 million) and Mick Jagger (143rd with £150 million), all of whom are principally performers and composers but make more than a little on the side from management. Admittedly, several of the 23 have made a proportion of their total wealth from other interests – property, retailing, investment and so on; and admittedly several of them inherited a fair proportion of their wealth – but that usually means their predecessors were dab hands at the management of creativity, too. On the other side of the balance sheet, a goodly number of individuals who have made tidy sums from the management of creativity were not on the list, or were listed as being in another kind of business because that is their principal source of income. Here, in alphabetical order, are the lucky 23:

	£million	Position	
Richard Branson	£1200	10th	Entertainment, travel and retail
Viscount Rothermere and family	£1000	14th	Newspaper publishing
Viscount Cowdray and family	£820	23rd	Media and land
Subhash Chandra	£450	40th	Media and entertainment
Bernard Lewis and family	£400	45th	Fashion and property
David Sullivan	£400	45th	Publishing and football
Lord Lloyd-Webber	£350	54th	Music
Sir Cameron Mackintosh	£350	54th	Entertainment
Lord Hamlyn	£275	75th	Publishing

Thomson family	£252	85th	Publishing
Felix Dennis	£250	87th	Publishing
Tom Singh	£200	108th	Fashion
Robert Stigwood	£200	108th	Entertainment
Andrew Brownsword	£190	122nd	Greetings cards
Lord Stockton and family	£175	131st	Publishing
Peter Simon and family	£155	141st	Fashion
Michael Heseltine	£150	143rd	Publishing
Saatchi Brothers	£140	163rd	Advertising
Chris Blackwell	£125	181st	Music
Douglas Graham and family	£125	181st	Newspaper publishing
Brian DeZille and family	£120	187th	Fashion
Freddie Johnston and family	£120	187th	Newspaper publishing
Paul Smith	£120	187th	Fashion

When I composed this chart for the earlier edition of this book in 1989, there were only 13 people in creative industries listed among the richest 200, well under 10%. Eight of that original 13 have remained in the top 200 throughout the decade. The other 15 in the above list are newcomers to this particular hall of fame. The last ten years have treated those in the creative industries very nicely, as might have been expected from everything said in the Introduction about their growth.

Having got this far with *Tantrums and Talent* you might be excused for thinking that they richly deserve every penny of their wealth, because managing creators is so painful. Not so. They may well deserve every penny of their wealth because managing creators is so difficult; or because the creative industries are so fiercely competitive and the ability to manage creators is so rare; or because managing creators is so taxing, demanding and exhausting. But not because it is painful. Not one of the managers of creativity who have contributed to this book find it anything but exciting, enjoyable and exhilarating. This may be because they are all exceptionally good at it, and people naturally tend to enjoy doing the things they are good at. Equally, they probably would not have dedicated their careers to the management of creativity had they found it a dreadful drudge. As was suggested in Chapter 5, those individuals who gain great pleasure from creativity gravitate towards the creative industries. (Those who do not gain great pleasure from creativity who, inadvertently, find themselves working in a creative industry shift themselves out pretty damn quickly.)

Without question the managers who work in creative industries enjoy gratifications unavailable in any other walks of life, and know they do. As leading business writer William Davis puts it:

> Innovation is surely the most exciting part of business life. It can also be one of the most frustrating. It can wreck careers is well as make them. But

there is nothing to compare with the thrill of finding a new idea and turning it into reality.

Creativity being a people business, it is hardly surprising that much of the thrill comes directly from working with creators:

I feel terribly lucky to be in this profession because the people I deal with, difficult as they are, and neurotic as they are, are interesting and fulfilling in lots of ways.

(Paul Hamlyn)

Sometimes you take a gamble with somebody – 'I like the way he talked about a programme, I think this person has got a bit of creative flair' – and you put them in the job. Then you watch them blossom and they come through with some marvellous ideas. Watching them grow, and get confidence, and maturity of judgment – that's a great feeling.

(Michael Grade)

Their generation of ideas is fantastically stimulating. With the very best creative people they introduce you to a way of looking at something which is totally different to the way you yourself look at it, so they open your horizons. The really great creative people are marvellous to work with.

(Tim Bell)

To be part of the creative process just makes me feel good.

(Chris Jones)

But if people are the source of most of the joys, they are also the source of most of the woes:

Pretentiousness and preciousness drive me mad. Creative people who feel that in some way, shape or form they do not necessarily have to subscribe to normal rules of human behaviour – that's the thing I cannot tolerate. Someone who is driving from A to B on location and insists he doesn't share a car, because his contract says he gets sole use of the car – it's a misuse of resources, a misuse of power, a misunderstanding of the entire process. It's destructive. The great talents don't have those pretentious qualities. Those pretentious qualities are armour, which moderately talented people surround themselves with to hide their insecurities.

(David Puttnam)

The most irritating aspects of working with creative people are their arrogance, their egotism and their total self-centredness, their feeling that the world has to revolve around them, that time doesn't exist, that time is their property: their complete selfishness in relation to other human beings. That is the worst conceivable aspect of working with creative people, that they are babyish and selfish. They are not all like that, only a small minority are like that, and if anybody behaves to them as they behave to other people they are bitterly resentful. If they are young and immature emotionally, which they frequently are, and if they become successful very quickly, the pitiful remnants of any self-discipline that may have been drilled into them at school or at home disappear totally and they become completely unmanageable.

(Wally Olins)

Wally Olins' word picture of some of the less attractive aspects of the creative personality mirrors the portrait delineated in Chapter 3. And the fact that creators need to be endlessly reassured, flattered, massaged and cuddled has already been discussed at length. In the end, happily, the ecstasies greatly outweigh the agonies. The bewitching enchantment of enabling creators to create obliterates the petty irritations and irksomeness of coping with their personality problems. Here then, are the self-defined job satisfactions of people in love with their work:

Whenever I've felt that the logistics of a job were getting me down – not another set of board minutes to approve, or another executive committee meeting to attend, or not another boring pile of correspondence to deal with – whenever I feel anything like that, I just talk to a designer or a director and they will convey by the enthusiasm of their response the excitement that they feel about the particular project they are working on. You suddenly feel the whole thing is worthwhile because the pleasure you are getting from your job is precisely that of enabling them to do what it is that they can do well; you feel you are almost giving birth to something, or rather acting as a sort of midwife, making a good thing possible that wouldn't have happened unless you had given the go-ahead. That is a huge reward and lifts one's job out of the ordinary. So the rewards of managing creativity are far greater than the strains and pressures.

(Jeremy Isaacs)

This amazing and unpredictable process sometimes results in work of which you are really proud, really glad to be associated with, really glad to see your company's name on. That's a terrific feeling, even if you only had an indirect involvement. It's like having a baby. My role, corporately, is that of the grandfather. I have a limited involvement, and far less of the pain. But even by association I take considerable pride, as the grandfather of the child. That's the greatest pleasure.

(Christopher Bland)

The pleasure for me is being part of a harmonious team who love working with each other and share a common dream. You see I actually love watching a great talent performing as part of a team. That's a great art, and great artists can do it – they sublimate themselves to the work in progress ... It is being part of something which is bigger than any individual, no matter how gifted. When you're working on a film that has something to say, everyone is swept along, it carries them, and you know you are part of something special.

(David Puttnam)

I adore it. This is a great gambling business, and I love it. It is full of surprises, daily. A publisher could not operate if he didn't like the excitement of a punt, even if he were in academic or educational publishing. One looks at something, one says this is right, one goes for it – and often you fall flat on your face. But when it works it's great.

(Paul Hamlyn)

It's marvellous to produce things that have made an impact on civilisation. It may only be a very small impact, it may only be a footnote, but it is an impact in social, cultural and economic terms. To take part in the development of the community as we are doing in a lot of our work, visually and culturally, is marvellous. I can't conceive of anything I would rather do.

(Wally Olins)

I do it for the buzz.

(Alan McGee)

But in all the thrills and spills, ups and downs, highs and lows of the creative manager's life, he must never forget the simple kernel of his *raison d'être*, which David Puttnam describes admirably:

One last thing. An original idea, a great idea, is God given. And an original idea is fragile, it can very, very easily get trampled on. The manager's job, first and foremost, is to protect the integrity of that original idea.

It is profitable, fun, and worthwhile. What more can you ask of a job?

Bibliography and References

The references mentioned in the text are to be found in the sources below:

Amabile, Teresa M. (1998) *How To Kill Creativity*, Harvard Business Review, September-October.

Argyle, Michael (1973) *Social Interaction,* Tavistock Publications.

Bach, Steven (1986) *Final Cut: Dreams and Disasters in the Making of* Heaven's Gate, Jonathan Cape Limited.

Badawy, Michael (1986) *How to Prevent Creativity Mismanagement*, Research Management, The Industrial Research Institute Inc.

Barron, F. (1969) *Creative Person and Creative Process*, Holt, Rinehart and Winston.

Birch, Paul & Clegg, Brian (1996) *Imagination Engineering*, Pittman Publishing.

Birtchnell, Richard, Targeting the Female Buyer – A Fashion Retailer's Perspective, speech given 24 January 1989.

Blanchard, K. & Johnson, S. (1983) *The One Minute Manager*, Fontana.

Bogen, Joseph E. (1969) *The Other Side of the Brain: an Appositional Mind*, Bulletin of the Los Angeles Neurological Society.

Bundy, Wayne M. (1997) *The Art of Discovery*, Crisp Publications Inc.

Charlotte, Susan (1993) *Creativity in Film*, Momentum Books.

Clark, R.W. (1984) *Einstein: The Life and Times*, Avon Books.

Cook, Peter (1998) *Best Practice Creativity*, Gower.

Coopersmith, S. (1967) *The Antecedents of Self-esteem*, Freeman.

Copyright, Design and Patents Act 1988, sections 77 and 80.

Crosbie, P.V. (Ed.) (1975) *Interaction in Small Groups*, Macmillan Publishing Co. Inc.

Csikszentmihalyi, M. & Getzels, J., *The Creative Vision: A Longitudinal Study of Problem Solving in Art*, John Wiley & Sons, 1976.

Culture, Business & Society Conference, Grosvenor House Hotel, 1 December 1997.

Davis, William (1989) *They All Laughed*, Global Business Magazine.

De Bono, Edward (1982) *Lateral Thinking for Management*, Penguin.

Deehan, G. & Evans, P. (1988) *The Keys to Creativity*, Grafton Books.

Design Council, *Creative Britain*, 31 March 1998.

Freud, Sigmund (1959) *Creative Writers and Daydreaming*, The Hogarth Press.

Garwood, D. (1964) Personality factors related to creativity in young scientists, *Journal of Abnormal and Social Psychology*, 68.

Gazzaniga, Michael S. (1985) *The Social Brain*, Basic Books.

Ghiselin, B. (Ed.) (1952) *The Creative Process*, Mentor Books.

Goldstein, M.L. (1985) Managing the Goldcollar Worker, *Industry Week*.

Gordon, W.J.J. (1961) *Synectics*, Harper & Row.

Gough, H.G., Identifying the Creative Man, *Journal of Value Engineering*, 2(4).

Gruber, Howard E. & Wallace, Doris B., (Eds.) (1989) *Creative People at Work*, Oxford University Press.

Haines, Bruce (1997) Managing Creatives, in *Excellence in Advertising*, Institute of Practitioners in Advertising.

Handy, Charles (1989) *The Age of Unreason*, Hutchinson.

Harding, R.E.M. (1940) *An Anatomy of Inspiration*, W. Heffer.

Hoffman, Paul (1988) *The Man Who Loved Only Numbers*, Fourth Estate.

Jervis, Paul (1998) *Leading the Continuously Creative Enterprise*, Royal Society of Arts.

Kirkwood, W.B. (1983) *The Search for Good Ideas*. Supervisory Management: The American Management Association.

Koestler, Arthur (1964) *The Act of Creation*, Hutchinson.

Leff, L.J., quoted in Anne Billson's review of *Hitchcock and Selznick*, *The Times*, April 15 1989.

Maslow, Abraham (1970) *A Theory of Human Motivation*, Penguin.

Maslow, Abraham (1973) *The Farther Reaches of Human Nature*, Harmondsworth.

McClintick, D. (1982) *Indecent Exposure*, William Morrow & Company.

Morris, Desmond (1962) *The Biology of Art*, Methuen.

Meiklejohn, Vince (1997) *The Management of Creative Staff in Advertising*, MBA Dissertation, University of Edinburgh.

Myerson, Jeremy (1999) Britain's most creative offices, *Management Today*, April.

National Advisory Committee on Creative and Cultural Education (1998) *Creative and Cultural Education: Towards a New Renaissance*, December.

National Endowment for Science (1998) *Technology and the Arts*, Consultation Paper, December.

Necton, S. (1985) *How to Spark New Ideas*, Nation's Business, US Chamber of Commerce.

Nokes, Barbara (1989) reported in *Campaign* magazine, 9 June.

Ocean, Humphrey & Tchalenko, John (1999) *The Painter's Eye*, National Portrait Gallery.

Ornstein, Robert (1972) *Psychology of Consciousness*, WH Freeman & Co.

Osborn, Alex F (1957) *Applied Imagination*, Charles Scribner's Sons.

Paris Review Interviews (1985) *Writers at Work*, Secker and Warburg.

Poltrack, Terence (1991) Stalking the Big Idea, *Agency* magazine, May–June.

Puttnam, David, (1989) in *Time* magazine, 1 May.

Prince, G.M. (1970) *The Practice of Creativity*, Macmilllan & Co, Inc.

Raudsepp, E. (1980) *Nurturing Managerial Creativity*, Dalton Communications Inc.

Rawlinson, J.G. (1951) *Creative Thinking and Brainstorming*, John Wiley and Sons.

Reber, A.S. (1985) *The Penguin Dictionary of Psychology*, Penguin.

Rooks, R. (1982) Creativity and conformity: finding the balance, *Management World*.

Russell, Bertrand (1965) *Portraits from Memory and Other Essays*, Allen & Unwin.

Stasinos, D. (1984) Enhancing the creative potential and self-esteem of mentally handicapped Greek children, *Journal of Creative Behaviour*, 18.

Sternberg, Robert J. (Ed.) (1988) *The Nature of Creativity*, Cambridge University Press.

Storr, Anthony (1972) *The Dynamics of Creation*, Secker and Warburg.

Storr, Anthony (1988) *The School of Genius*, Andre Deutsch.

Sveiby, Karl Erik & Lloyd, Tom (1987) *Managing Know How*, Bloomsbury.

The Rich List 1999, The *Sunday Times*, 11 April 1999.

Townsend, Robert (1970) *Up The Organisation*, Michael Joseph.

Weeks, D.J. with Ward, K. (1988) *Eccentrics: The Scientific Investigation*, Stirling University Press.

Weisberg, R.W. (1986) *Creativity: Genius and Other Myths*, WH Freeman & Co.

Weiss, B. (1986) *Hiring Creative People*, Personnel Administrator: American Society for Personnel Administration.

Zeldman, Maurice I. (1980) How management can develop and sustain a creative Environment, *SAM Advanced Management Journal*.

Index